ACTING

ACTING
THOUGHT *into* ACTION

REVISED EDITION

Kurt Daw

Illustrations by
Rosemary Ingham and Lawren Spera

HEINEMANN ■ Portsmouth, NH

Heinemann
A division of Reed Elsevier Inc.
361 Hanover Street
Portsmouth, NH 03801–3912
www.heinemanndrama.com

3 1969 02536 8605

Offices and agents throughout the world

The author and publisher wish to thank those who have generously given permission to reprint borrowed material:

Figure 1.2: Photograph courtesy of Jack Pleasants.
Figure 1.5: Photograph by Joan Marcus courtesy of Arena Stage.
Figures 2.1, 2.2, and 2.3: Photographs courtesy of the Billy Rose Theatre Collection, The New York Public Library for the Performing Arts, Astor, Lenox, and Tilden Foundations.
Figure 8.2: Photograph by Richard Feldman courtesy of Arena Stage.
Page 63: "Portrait of Igor Stravinsky" by Pablo Picasso, 1920. Copyright © 1997 by the Estate of Pablo Picasso/Artists Rights Society (ARS), New York.

Library of Congress Cataloging-in-Publication Data
Daw, Kurt.
    Acting : thought into action / Kurt Daw ; illustrations by Rosemary Ingham and Lawren Spera.—Rev. ed.
        p. cm.
    Includes bibliographical references and index.
    ISBN 0-325-00620-2 (alk. paper)
    1. Acting.   2. Method (Acting).   I. Title.

PN2061.D38 2004
792.02'8—dc22   2004005741

Editor: Lisa A. Barnett
Production: Vicki Kasabian
Cover design: Jenny Jensen Greenleaf
Author photograph: Mimi Fitipaldi
Typesetter: Tom Allen, Pear Graphic Design
Manufacturing: Jamie Carter

Printed in the United States of America on acid-free paper
08 07 06 05 04   M-V   1 2 3 4 5

To my wife, Hillary,
and my son, David,
for their love
and support

Contents

Acknowledgments

Many friends and colleagues contributed both help and encouragement to both this edition and the first edition of this book. I owe a debt to my many acting teachers, especially Forrest Sears, Jack Clay, and the late Margaret Neiwirth. A particular stimulus to thinking about the problems of contemporary acting theory came from a summer seminar on American approaches to Stanislavski, organized by Jack Clay at the University of Washington in 1988.

I want to thank my students at Kennesaw State University and The State University of New York at New Paltz. Julia Matthews, Karen Robinson, and Frank Trezza were especially generous colleagues over the years, whom I thank for their friendship and support.

Bob and Rosemary Ingham, who have known me since I was a student, took me seriously when I first said I had an interest in writing this book, read early drafts, and treated the project with respect and encouragement long before there was enough substance to justify their faith. I miss Bob tremendously and still hold Rosemary as my role model of what I wish to be as a teacher and a colleague in the theatre.

My friends and colleagues from the Association for Theatre in Higher Education (ATHE) and my particular home within that organization, Theatre as a Liberal Art (TLA), continue to provide inspiration, good company, and plenty of discussion about acting and theatre. Many of them have adopted this book in their classrooms and offered me ongoing insights into its reception by their students and how it might be improved.

I received incalculable professional support and help from Lisa Barnett and Vicki Kasabian at Heinemann.

Sonny Stokes provided me with vital insights into myself, acting, and theatre in New York. Like so many artists, my life has been vastly improved because of having known her.

Finally, I wish to thank my family. I am indebted to my parents and brothers. I especially thank my father-in-law, Thomas Hight, who has treated me like a son, shown continued interest in my work, and given valuable feedback about my theories from the perspective of a layperson. Along with my late mother-in-law, Jean, he has provided long-term support of my education and career.

In the decade since I first drafted this book, I have had nearly daily conversations about it, acting, and theatre with my wife, Hillary, who is my best friend and closest collaborator. My son, David, has grown into a fine young man and a talented actor. His interest in my work as he independently studied acting has led to the most interesting and insightful conversations of my life. There are no words that can begin to measure their contribution or thank them enough.

Preface

I wrote this book because, as an actor and an acting teacher, I needed to find a better way to discuss my craft. I have long been struck by how difficult it is to *talk* about acting. I don't mean trading theatre stories, which is both easy and fun. But it is extremely hard to discuss with other actors what we do and how we do it. Our vocabulary can't describe all the subtle mental activities involved in performance. Because of the basic intangibility of acting—its subjective and personal nature—there isn't any easy way to describe our processes to one another.

Like most actors of my generation, I was trained in an American derivation of the Stanislavski system, and when I wished to discuss acting I did so in the hand-me-down metaphors through which the system is commonly explained—as do most actors, I discovered over the years. I also soon discovered that there are rival loyalties to particular metaphors that are, ironically, trying to express the same underlying phenomena. One school says, *Act before you think.* Another says, *Don't act, react.* Yet another says, *Live the part.* I have witnessed many discussions of the acting process turn sour as actors disagree about the aptness of the metaphors, as if these were the thing itself.

As I used and taught the system over the years, I became more concerned that the usual elucidations about *why* the system worked were all based in metaphor. The result was that many of the things we told ourselves and our students weren't true. (I don't mean to quibble with the intent of metaphorical explanation, but as one example, if what we mean by *Act before you think* is to do something without the involvement of your brain, it is impossible.)

Stanislavski himself recognized this problem and sought to find scientific definition in the resources available in his lifetime. Most of the mechanical explanations suggested as possible by Stanislavski, however, have proven over time to lack scientific validity, and subsequent research has done little to improve the situation. As an educator I was concerned about repeating the same old metaphoric explanations when I knew most of them to be nothing but "plausible stories" at best and downright antiquated and discarded science at worst.

My own crisis came one day when a student asked me, after completing an exercise, *"Precisely what happens* when one does this work?" I realized I didn't know, and I wasn't sure that anyone else did.

This book is the result of my trying to find out. I can't say that I yet know all, or even most, of the answers. I have learned a lot, however, from my colleagues and friends in the cognitive sciences who have been remarkably interested and helpful. I have explored many avenues, some not immediately connected to theatre. Readers familiar with Betty Edwards' remarkable *Drawing on the Right Side of the Brain* will recognize its influence throughout this book, though that work deals with theatre not at all. I am also indebted to the works of Susanne Langer and her spiritual successor, Howard Gardner, for their explorations of the arts and their relation to mental life.

In this work, I postulate a thought pyramid that I use to simplify and summarize a number of similar but very distinct approaches to mapping the mind. I make reference in the text to Gardner's multiple intelligences theory, the right brain/left brain phenomenon, and the bottom-up versus top-down approach that is a constant part of artificial intelligence discussions. I recognize that by blurring them I am diluting each individual argument. But since I am primarily interested in their application to acting, I have focused on their two great points of commonality, which are (1) the validation of the existence of an alternate perceptual mode and (2) the recognition of layers of thought, some of which lie below the level of conscious recognition.

This book is unapologetically Stanislavskian in its approach, in part because his is the only theory of acting that is both comprehensive and objective. Stanislavski was not promoting a particular approach to acting, but instead was defining *what it is.* His system was an attempt to codify the approaches that good actors had always used. I, in turn, am not proposing a new theory of actor training. I am only trying to explain (with knowledge unavailable to Stanislavski) why his training system works as it does and perhaps to suggest some subtle refocusing as a result of understanding the operations of the pieces better.

I wanted the book to be easy to use. For example, the Contents includes the major headings in each chapter so that you can check back while working on any specific section to see where that piece fits in the overall picture. Since an acting book is usually a long-term resource, consulted again and again, the expanded Contents makes it easier for you to dip into the book quickly, find the section or exercise you are looking for, re-read it, place it in context, and get back to work.

Throughout the book, you'll find highlighted quotations from actors and other theatre practitioners. These statements reinforce the significance of a particular idea or concept and guide you to additional material you may want to pursue (the sources are listed in the notes). I encourage you to add your own notes, underlinings, highlights, and quotations. Use the book as a kind of minijournal. (And remember the old actor's trick of dating your notes so you can later trace the evolution of your thought.)

I should also mention two minor technical points. I use the secondary spelling *wholistic* rather than the preferred *holistic* because I find the meaning to be clearer and more provocative. This is, after all, a book about using one's whole brain. I also fretted about how to deal with Stanislavski's name, since it is variously spelled (Constantine, Constantin, Konstantin, Stanislavsky, Stanislavski) in the many sources I have consulted and quoted. To avoid confusion, I decided to regularize all spellings of the name to the form adopted by Jean Benedetti in his authoritative biography. (The only exceptions are in the notes and recommended reading when a different spelling appears in a book title.)

Finally, a few words about format. Historically, acting texts were ersatz novels, stories of the training of fictional students. The astute reader could deduce the step-by-step processes, but the format was not very conducive to conveying technical information. More recently, acting texts have borrowed the very specific instructions of self-help books. (Many books, in fact, have become exercise encyclopedias.) Unfortunately, these instructions are often more confusing than enlightening to anyone who is not sitting in a classroom with the author. Exercises have a way of playing out along many different lines of development.

Since either approach is unsatisfactory on its own, I have attempted to incorporate the best of each. The exercises are introduced in short, descriptive sequences. An evaluation section then summarizes the typical result. This in turn is followed by a story, a fiction, of one or two practical attempts at the work. Some examples are of successes, some of failures. Either way, the aim is to help the reader imagine some of the ways the exercises may play out. (By the way, the exercise work in this book begins in Chapter 4. You can skip straight there after Chapter 1 if you wish. Chapters 2 and 3 give some background on what you are going to do, but you can read them at your convenience. If you want to work on the exercises first, and return to the theory later, feel free.)

This is a book for those who want to learn to act, whether that be for their own enjoyment or in preparation for a career. It is based on observations about the way real actors do their work in real circumstances. It relates traditional ideas that have been the subject of public discussion for decades to recent information about how the mind works. It focuses on the role of creativity in the art of acting. Its aim is to release in the actor the potential ability that is already there and allow that ability to be mastered. Above all, I hope this book will help make it easier to *think* and *talk* about the thing I love so much, the art and craft of the actor.

◢ Note for Teachers

Although this book is primarily intended for the general reader, it can also be used as a classroom textbook. The exercises are already sequenced. Several chapters end with additional related exercises, if you want to spend more time on a particular skill. What cannot be supplied by a book, of course, is the wisdom and experience you bring to a classroom as a teacher.

Recent research suggests that there is much you can do to help students understand and accomplish the process of shifting to the creative state. Mihaly Csikszentmihalyi, a University of Chicago professor of psychology, has outlined five Cs—conditions that contribute to optimal experience in education. Creating these five conditions is largely within the control of the instructor. They are listed on the next few pages, with a few suggestions about what they mean in relation to the exercises in this book.

Clarity

The more specific you can be about the goal of an exercise, the better students will be able to accomplish it. Particularly in teaching the early exercises in this book (in Chapters 4 through 7) you can help students by clarifying that they are working on *the feel of the creative state,* not on making an impression to an audience. More often than not, what goes wrong in early training is that students concentrate too much on the external impact of their acting (their public success) and too little on the internal process. I have witnessed many classes where the main goal seemed to be to speak loudly and face front—at least, that was all the teacher commented on. There will certainly come a time for that, but not in the first lessons. Be clear that you are teaching a style of mental processing.

Centering

You must focus on the students' work in the present moment—their concrete experiences and immediate reactions to them—rather than their grades, jobs, or careers. This does not mean that you shouldn't care about what happens to them in the long run. However, they need guidance on the spot. They need to sense that what they are doing right now is more important than what it may gain them in the future. In an acting class, this means they need side-coaching while they are working more than they need written evaluations and grades handed out in the next class. You may choose to do both, that's fine, but don't neglect the first for the second.

This is often difficult for teachers because the pressures of the academy and student expectations can make the letter grade seem all-important. It is, however, immensely meaningful to creative artists when they know it is them, personally, not grades, about which we care most. You may want to hold off grading the first few exercises. You should also be prepared for the issue to rear its head every time there is a final grade or deadline.

Choice

Students need to have choices available to them. They will learn more and do better if they may choose when to work, even if there are stern penalties for failing to work. Contrary to conventional classroom wisdom, this means we should not structure exercise and performance requirements too tightly. It is common to assign a day to work on exercises or scene performances and even go so far as to post a performance order. However, students will be more likely to have an optimal experience if they have some say in the matter. The best teacher I ever studied with used to ask simply, "Who wants to work?" We all knew that if we didn't work at least every few days, and on certain predetermined performance days, we would receive a lower grade or possibly flunk. On the other hand, we *chose* when to work. It was never coerced or forced on us. There were a couple of long pauses early on. One day I heard that no one had volunteered in another class and the instructor had said, "Okay, let's go home. Do what you need to do to get ready for the next class," and dismissed everyone. It takes courage as an instructor to give your students this freedom/responsibility, but it pays off. From this experience I learned how to take responsibility for myself as an artist. It nurtured the sense that I acted because I wanted to, not because I had to. It also led me to structure a regimen for preparing myself. Your students will benefit from this, too. (Choice is particularly important in relation to the performance exercises in Chapters 8 and 12.)

Commitment

Commitment is the trust that enables students to put aside self-consciousness and fear of failure and try. It is the discipline they use when attempting new approaches. If you are committed to creating a welcoming learning environment, your students will be able to commit to learning the craft. The environment of trust must be created early and diligently guarded, but the greatest challenges to it will come during the partner work in conjunction with Chapters 9 and 10.

Challenge

Students need to be challenged by a sequenced series of experiences, each of which stretches students to try a little harder or to do a little more. At the same time, it is important that the exercises not be beyond their capabilities or they will only feel frustration. We all know this is the hardest part of teaching, especially when a class is made up of students at many different levels. It takes great sensitivity to each individual student to gauge how far to push and how much to support. This book offers a sequence, but you can greatly increase the effectiveness of the sequence by monitoring the pace. The exercises build on one another. As an instructor you can decide when to spend more time on an exercise, when a student needs to back up and review a fundamental skill, and when it is time to move along to the next exercise. As a rule of thumb, take plenty of time with the work outlined in Chapters 4 through 8, and work a bit more quickly after that.

These are, of course, very general guidelines. Your experience and intuition as a teacher can help you gauge how to proceed. I would be most interested in your experience in using these exercises. If you have comments or questions, please feel free to write to me in care of the publisher.

BACKGROUND

1 Thinking Like an Actor

Bringing to life a character's words, actions, and ideas in the theatre is one of the most exciting, enriching, and liberating experiences in the world. Discovering a process by which you can bring a character to life is the task of the student actor, and mastering it can be very surprising. Learning to act turns out to be very different than most students imagine it. It is at once both less mystical and less logical than you probably anticipate it will be.

> *The words on the page are only clues to the life boiling underneath them.*
> *—Zelda Fichandler*

It is less mystical in that you will discover actors do not have some special, inborn, extra talent: they use skills we all have, but they do so in a specific and concentrated way. It is less logical in that they have learned to think in a strikingly counterintuitive way that allows them to elude stereotypical expression and conventional representation. Most people never become competent actors, not because they lack talent but because they do not understand the nature of their skills and, therefore, cannot con-

> *[Acting is] a matter of thinking. . . . It's a matter of becoming aware of what it is you're doing, of what it is you're feeling, and then it's a matter of controlling it any way you want with your brain.*
> *—Anne Bancroft*

trol them. Ironically, it is not what they lack that impedes them but rather the extra baggage of which they cannot rid themselves.

The basic skill needed to act is *frame of mind*. It is simply *a different way of thinking*. Good acting is built upon working in this unique mindset. The first great acting teacher of modern times, Konstantin Stanislavski, called this mental mode the "creative state of mind." The first step toward learning to act is really the process of learning to think like an actor.

Unfortunately this is difficult to learn to do from descriptions in a book. For this reason, most acting books are not for beginners. They can help a great deal once you have built a firm foundation by learning to put yourself in a creative state of mind, but about this first step you have been pretty much on your own. This book is different. It *is* for absolute beginners. It does not presuppose that you know anything about acting. It explains the very first things an actor must do, starting with the fundamental skill of thinking like an actor.

The difficulty in learning this first step is that any thought process, including this alternate one, is so intangible. The problem in teaching and learning acting has always been that although it is possible to discuss *what* to do, we lack a way to describe *how* to do it. Thinking, including thinking in the alternate mode of the actor, is very subjective. The experience is internal. It is almost impossible to learn from simple observation, because any reasonably competent performance is marked by the appearance of spontaneous creation: the artistry that created it is concealed.

> In all of the vast acting literature—the textbooks, the memoirs, the anecdotes, the biographies and auto-biographies, the interviews, the historical studies, the theoretical speculations, the manifestos—it is rare to find any mention of what acting feels like. What could be more important than to know what it is like to be there, on stage or before a camera?
> —Richard Hornby

Acting is also very difficult to learn by asking questions, because even willing teachers find the process is very difficult to put into words. It is not that actors are not generous in attempting to explain their work, but to the uninitiated their answers seem so understated or mystical as to be meaningless. They say things like *Acting is reacting* or *Become the character,* which, of course, explain nothing at all.

Eventually nearly everyone learns how to engage the actor's thought process through trial and error. A few students stumble upon a process for themselves remarkably quickly. They just *get it*, seemingly overnight. For most, however, this is a long and painful process. Many never master it. They give up, thinking themselves "untalented."

Another Way of Thinking

Recent advances in cognitive neuroscience, and in the teaching of other fields of art, have intimated to us that Stanislavski's "creative state of mind" is actually just an alternate manner of mental processing, particularly of sensory information. Actors, it seems, think in an *alternate perceptual mode* that is quite foreign to the classroom or, for that matter, to any conscious "thinking."

This mode is similar to but separate from logic. It is a process of bringing together information and arranging it into a coherent pattern, but in a freewheeling and instinctive way. Only recently have we developed enough information about this way of thinking to begin to put it into words reliably. Once we understood more about this mode, however, we discovered it is much more common in everyday experience than anyone had suspected. *All of us occasionally find ourselves in this alternate perceptual mode, but few of us ever learn to control it consciously, giving rise to the myth that it is a special inborn talent.* Once you know more about it you will no doubt be able to think of many common activities, such as drawing (Figure 1.1), meditation (Figure 1.2), and sports (Figure 1.3), that put you in an alternate perceptual state.

Your Own Alternate State

Each of us sometimes slips off into an alternate mode of thought. This is precisely what daydreaming is, for example. You may find yourself engrossed in a project—working on a craft, cooking, drawing, reading, and even just planning—that commands your concentration and seems to put you off in your own world. If you have ever lost track of time, you know what being in an alternate mode of thought feels like. Probably, however, you did not consciously *induce* this state; it just slipped up on you.

If you reflect on these times, you will also note that they are the moments in your life when you have been most creative. Although you lost track of the world, your problem or activity became very

Figure 1.1. Stephen Ingham, drawing

clear and you accomplished a great deal toward solving it. These times are very productive.

You can learn to control this way of thinking, even if you think of yourself as inartistic or uncreative. It does not require special talent or extraordinary ability. When you learn this different way of using your brain, you will enrich your life enormously. Before we can start, however, we need to talk about what acting is and isn't.

What Acting Isn't

The greatest obstacle most beginning actors face is coming to understand what they are supposed to do. Many have a major conceptual

Figure 1.2. Sandra Pleasants, yoga instructor

Figure 1.3. Hong Qiao, playing table tennis

Figure 1.4. Nineteenth-century acting poses

misunderstanding that impedes their progress. They believe they are supposed to explain the story to the audience.

But acting isn't explaining. Audiences understand the meaning of the words. They do not need to see the actor touch his heart when he says the word *love,* they do not need to hear the actor suddenly shift to a low guttural growl when she speaks the word *bad,* they do not need actors to illustrate all their verbs with demonstrations. Acting is certainly about performing a special role in relationship to the words of the play, but that role is not meant to serve as a living dictionary.

Contrary to tabloid implications, acting is not a matter of just looking good, either. Despite the way that teen idols are relentlessly sold to us as physical commodities, many great actors are a long way from exemplifying physical perfection. You can be a successful actor no matter how you look.

Nor is acting a matter of good diction, good posture, or superior intellect. These things play a part in an actor's training, because they can be used to improve a performance, but they are not at the core of acting. Concentrating on them too heavily can preclude ever getting to the core. In the latter part of the nineteenth century actors studied stock poses and gestures to indicate emotion (the drawings in Figure 1.4 are taken from a text published in 1898). But acting isn't posing, indicating, or possessing extraordinary beauty. The power of a performance—Zelda Rubenstein's in *The*

Figure 1.5. Zelda Rubenstein as Charlotta in the Arena Theater's production of The Cherry Orchard *by Anton Chekhov*

Cherry Orchard, for example (see Figure 1.5)—lies in its intensity and focus.

Acting is not about surface appearances at all! Anything that smacks of adjusting one's appearance creates an artificiality about the performance that observers find vain and distancing. We all know this from our experiences with being photographed. Somehow the more aware we are that our picture is being taken the worse it gets. Given time to adjust our hair, fix our clothes, correct our posture, and assume an attitude, we somehow manage to appear stilted and fake. The most natural pictures of us are always candid shots we didn't know were being taken. Even with hair out of place, rumpled clothes, and slack posture, we seem more alive and interesting.

Acting is not explaining

What Acting Is

Acting is creating a sense of life. It is giving an audience an experience so vivid and truthful that it is revelatory. All plays have this in common, whether or not they are realistic. The great common denominator of theatre is the sense of life: it is spontaneously created at the instant the audience sees it, and as it is lived in front of their eyes the humanity of the subject matter comes through.

Actors create this sense of life not by manipulating appearances, but by experiencing the action as it occurs. They are in the "here and now," a state where concentration on the details of the moment preclude the distractions of the past or future. In this sense, they have a great deal in common with those other "players," athletes.

What You Will Learn in This Book

Acting is a wholistic competence, composed of a very small number of constituent skills. The building block for all these skills is the ability to recognize and control an alternate mental mode. This book is structured to help you learn first how to enter this "creative state" and then to develop the first seven skills of the actor. In a

---

Some well-known definitions of acting

Living truthfully in imaginary circumstances.
—Sanford Meisner, paraphrasing Stanislavski

The combination of unusual sensitivity and extraordinary intelligence.
—French actor Francois-Joseph Talma

The ability to react to imaginary stimuli. —Lee Strasberg

Learning the laws of your own responsiveness.
—Actor/teacher John Lehne

The ability to create and to respond to imaginary objects and circumstances. —Harold Clurman

Nothing more or less than playing. The idea is to humanize life.
—Jeff Goldblum

series of short, focused lessons you will learn to master each of these skills, and in the end, to integrate them into the wholistic skill of acting.

These skills can be learned in a relatively short period of time. When used as a textbook, this series of lessons is ordinarily taught in one ten-week quarter or fifteen-week semester. Like other wholistic skills, for example driving, drawing, or playing a sport, the experience of learning the constituent skills can seem daunting at first, but it will actually develop quickly. Once you have learned each skill, you will have it forever. The best news is that the fundamentals of acting comprise only this small set of skills. You will not have to go on adding more and more basic skills forever. At the end of this series of lessons you will have a full arsenal. You may choose to study advanced acting further, but you will have already mastered the basics and they will serve you for the rest of your life.

The First Seven Skills

The skills you will learn are packaged into seven basic lessons and two related performances in which groups of exercises are integrated into a larger skill. These lessons are:

A matter of giving away secrets. —Ellen Barkin

Supplying truthful feelings under unnatural circumstances.
—Alexander Pushkin

A celebration of the fact that we contain within ourselves infinite possibilities. —Daniel Day-Lewis

Dealing with very delicate emotions. It is not putting up a mask. Each time an actor acts he does not hide; he exposes himself.
—Jeanne Moreau

Not being emotional, but being able to express emotion.
—Thomas Reid

The most immediate way in which a human being can share with another the sense of what it is to be a human being.
—Thornton Wilder

- *Relaxation.* Getting physically and mentally ready to act by eliminating distractions and excess baggage.
- *Actor's concentration.* Learning to recognize, induce and control the actor's perceptual mode, and how to use this *creative state*.
- *Creating given circumstances.* The most common definition of acting is "living truthfully in imaginary circumstances." This lesson teaches you how to leverage the creative state to help create a physical and emotional reality on stage.
- *Adding speech.* Learning to add the element of speech without shifting back into the wrong mental mode.

Giving a solo performance. The first interlude, which integrates the previous four skills into a working whole.

- *Creating a relationship.* Using the previous skills while interacting with another actor.
- *Making choices.* Living in the moment through the element of choice.
- *Working with a text.* Understanding the script and how to analyze it.

Performing a scene with a partner. The final exercise, which integrates all the skills into a powerful performance.

Realism

The exercises in this book are designed to teach you to act realistically. You will learn to perform in a style in which you process information and behave as you would in the real world. To spectators, your performance has the look of the world in which they operate daily.

This is not to imply that realism is superior to other performance styles. It is only a point of departure. By learning realism, you will master the fundamental principles of acting, which you can then extrapolate for other styles. In this sense, realism becomes a means to an end, not an end in itself.

There are important reasons for beginning with realism, however. The first is that realism remains the dominant style of performance in our time, particularly in film and television. The second is that learning to act realistically builds confidence in the validity of the performance. Knowing that you can create an illusion that is believable when measured against an objective criterion (reality) is far more powerful than just feeling that your performance was a success. Beginners working in abstract styles frequently feel little more than that they "got away with it." An accomplished realistic performance objectively confirms that the work is good. Finally, realism is the style that most deeply uses the alternate perceptual mode of the actor. It is fundamental. All other styles employ varying degrees of abstraction.

Getting Started

The next two chapters of the book give you a theoretical background about acting. The first of these discusses the foundations of modern acting by looking at the man who codified the fundamental approach to training actors, Konstantin Stanislavski, and his legacy. The second looks at the cognitive research that led to the theory that underlies the training method used in this book. Most students find these chapters very helpful in understanding what they are about to do, but they may be read later without harming the work. Feel free to leap ahead to Chapter 4 to start the exercises. When you are ready to think in more traditional ways about acting theory, Chapters 2 and 3 will give you enough information to get you started and to contextualize the work. The Resources section at the end of the book will lead you to further resources to continue your exploration.

Record of Progress

As you work your way through this book you will find it very beneficial to keep a record of what you are doing:

1. As soon as you begin to perceive like an actor, you will lose sight of what it was like not to. Without a clear record, you may not be able to see your progress. Too often, artists get trapped in self-destructive cycles because they always focus on their shortcomings, however small, not on their improvement. A good record will confirm your progress.
2. Most artistic problems surface again and again throughout a career. A good record will help you recognize these recurrent cycles and help you solve the problems quickly and more easily.

Begin a journal now. It does not need to be formal. It is for you. It is a collection of your observations. It should include notes on the scenes or subjects on which you are currently working, what is happening in your life that is affecting your work, and new discoveries. *Exclude any negative self-evaluations of your performance.* These are often distorted and inaccurate, and they strengthen the depression/perfection cycle that is so destructive.

Write down your questions about the acting process. Nothing will confirm your progress as quickly as reading through old notes in which you pondered how to do something before discovering the answer.

If you can, prepare a short monologue and record it. This can be accomplished the old-fashioned way on videotape but is increasingly easy to do with a computer. Although doing so may immediately raise your anxiety level, remember that the purpose of this recording is to give you objective information about your performance *before you had any instruction.* You cannot perform badly or "incorrectly"; anything you do will be an accurate reflection of your abilities at a point in time. This is the only purpose the record serves.

2 The Creative State of Mind

The search for an alternative mode of thought is not new in actor training. It is the basic impulse behind the Stanislavski system, the most widely influential of modern training movements, and the one that underlies most contemporary actor training.

Konstantin Stanislavski was the great Russian actor/director who cofounded the Moscow Art Theatre, an extraordinary acting company still in existence today. Stanislavski rose to fame as director and leading actor in the plays of Anton Chekhov.

Toward the midpoint of his career, in 1906, Stanislavski suffered a personal artistic crisis and lost confidence in his abilities. He realized his work had become inconsistent. Though he was sometimes magnificent, he was more often mundane. His inspiration had begun to elude him; even performances of his favorite roles became flat. He searched for a way to use conscious technique to induce the alternate state of mind that he had experienced during his world-renowned performances.

He retreated to his vacation home in Finland to contemplate how an actor does his work, drawing from his own considerable experience and his observations of some of the great artists of his time. Poring through journals covering over twenty years of work, he was able to discern and codify a set of principles that he used to improve

Figure 2.1. Konstantin Stanislavski (1863–1938) in a photo taken in 1924, while he was touring America

his own work. Later, he began to experiment with teaching these principles to young performers in a studio associated with his theatre. Through his work he demonstrated that acting is indeed capable of being taught, and the system he devised continues to form the basis of most actor training in educational institutions throughout the world.

The Inspired State

Observing himself in performance, Stanislavski realized that when he was in top form he was in a different condition. Acting was easy, almost effortless, creative, and relaxing. He called this condition the "creative state of mind." His terminology makes clear that he considered it a mental state, a way of thinking.

Nearly everyone who has spent time on stage has experienced this remarkable, euphoric state, even those who have often dismissed it as a by-product of an inspired moment. It was Stanislavski's proposition, and that of this book, that this state is

Figure 2.2. The actors of the Moscow Art Theatre, the company Stanislavski cofounded and raised to world renown—Stanislavski is in the front row, fourth from left

not a product of great acting *but its cause*. Nor need it be limited to a few scattered moments. It is possible to enter this state each time one acts. When Stanislavski set out to develop his principles for actor training, contemplation of this state and how to achieve it reliably guided his work.

Despite its centrality to his teachings, this is the least tangible, and therefore least understood, aspect of Stanislavski's scholarship. His ideas on this subject, decades ahead of their time, have until recently seemed almost mystical. Now, in light of contemporary brain research, this central tenet of Stanislavski's work can be explained, and perhaps understood, in a new way.

> *Every actor Stanislavski respected shared certain qualities: there was a kind of aura around them on the stage. They were relaxed yet filled with a concentrated energy. They were completely involved in the theatrical moment, possessing an ease and liveliness that gave each of their roles a special charge. Stanislavski called this inspired artistic condition the creative state of mind. —Mel Gordon*

Components of Acting

Stanislavski was active in many aspects of actor training, from exercises to theory, but his lasting contribution was the way he carefully observed inspired acting and then built a system committed to creating conditions that allowed it to occur.

Stanislavski deduced his set of principles by observing prominent actors of his time and carefully examining his own process while rehearsing and performing. He was aided by the new science of psychology, which gave him a vocabulary to discuss the internal, mental aspects of the work. *This ability to distinguish inner process from outer product has become the hallmark of his system.* He sought further inspiration from a wide variety of sources, including Eastern mysticism and Zen Buddhism.

Stanislavski noted that great acting is characterized by mental and physical relaxation, concentrated inventiveness, a lack of self-consciousness, and a powerful commitment to behaving truthfully within the imaginary world of the play. But what most fascinated him was that while in such a state, actors were so deeply involved in the work that they did not seem to be "acting" at all. They were easy and natural, reacting in ways far beyond conscious control. Stanislavski believed that the actor uses "conscious technique to tap the unconscious." Throughout his career Stanislavski remained intrigued by the uncanny manner in which actors were capable of delivering performances that went far beyond their conscious intentions.

What Stanislavski admired becomes

Let's start with the solemn measured gait of the actors. They do not walk, they advance across the stage, they do not sit, they ensconce themselves, they do not lie down, they recline, they do not stand, they adopt a pose. Agitation is expressed by pacing up and down the stage very quickly, by the hands being seen to tremble when a letter is being opened or by letting the jug knock against the glass and then the glass against the teeth when water is being poured and drunk. Illness—a hacking cough, the shivers, or vertigo (theatrical medicine only recognizes consumption, fever and anemia). Death—clutching the chest or tearing at one's shirt collar (the hack actor only recognizes two causes of death, cardiac arrest and asphyxia).
—Stanislavski, identifying the elements of bad acting

clearest when contrasted with what he disliked. He despised stock gestures, sign-language-like indication, mannered speaking, and slavish imitation of other performances.

Though no definitive outline of his work was ever set down, Stanislavski did on several occasions delineate a tentative series of discrete steps that could be used to train an actor to develop a creative state of mind. Although these lists of steps were not all identical, the following one, adapted from notes he published in 1921, contains the major elements common to most of them.

> *Stanislavski could not help asking himself whether there were not some technical ways of achieving the creative state of mind. That did not mean that he wanted to produce inspiration itself in some artificial way, for that he realized was impossible. What he wanted to find out was whether there was not some way of creating conditions favorable to the emergence of inspiration; an atmosphere in which inspiration was more likely to come to the actor.*
> —David Magarshack

An Outline of the Stanislavski System

1. *Relaxation.* Learning to relax the muscles and eliminate unnecessary physical tension while performing.
2. *Concentration.* Learning to think like an actor in an alternate perceptual mode and to respond to the stimulus of one's own imagination.
3. *Work with the senses.* Discovering the sensory base of the work: learning to memorize and recall sensations, often called *sense memory* and/or *affective memory;* learning to work from a small sensation and expand it, a technique Stanislavski called "spheres of attention." Discovering the sensory basis of both physical feeling and emotional feeling and their relationship.
4. *Sense of truth.* Learning to tell the difference between the organic and the artificial; Stanislavski believed that there were natural laws of acting, which were to be obeyed.
5. *Creating given circumstances.* Developing the ability to use the previous four skills to create, physically and emotionally, the reality of the world of the play (the circumstances given in the text and by the director) through true and organic means.

6. *Contact and communication.* Developing the ability to interact with other performers spontaneously, and with an audience, without violating the world of the play.
7. *Units and objectives.* Learning to divide the role into sensible units that can be worked on individually, and developing the ability to define each unit of the role by an active goal desired by the character rather than as an entirely literary idea.
8. *Logic and believability.* Discovering how to be certain that the sum of the combined objectives are consistent and coherent and that they are in line with the play as a whole.
9. *Work with the text.* Developing the ability to uncover the social, political, and artistic meaning of the text and seeing that these ideas are contained within the performance.
10. *The creative state of mind.* An automatic culmination of all the previous steps.

Stanislavski and Chekhov's Subtext

The plays of Anton Chekhov presented Stanislavski and his fellow actors at the Moscow Art School with a complicated acting problem. Scattered throughout Chekhov's major plays (*The Seagull, Uncle Vanya, Three Sisters,* and *The Cherry Orchard*) are scenes where the main plot points are conveyed through means other than dialogue. A simple example might be the scene near the end of *Three Sisters* where a character named Tusenbach holds a very trivial conversation with his fiancée, Irina, about coffee and a few items on his desk. The scene is utterly incomprehensible if you don't know that Tusenbach is on his way to fight a duel with a rival for Irina's affections that he suspects (correctly, as it turns out) he will not survive. This fact is never mentioned in the scene, and no explanation is ever made for the reason that Tusenbach utters such banalities instead of telling his love good-bye, perhaps forever. The words written for him to deliver at that point in the play have very little to do with the main plot interest at that moment. Commonly, we read into his psychology that he is unwilling or unable to utter the words out loud because he is unable to face his coming death. (Another such example is found in the scene from *The Seagull* analyzed in Chapter 11.)

Stanislavski's dramaturg, Vladimir Nemirovich-Danchenko, called these indirectly expressed plot points *subtext*.

Psychology was just developing at the time, so it was a new intellectual idea that people may have interior lives that they are not only unwilling, but sometimes unable, to express. Chekhov was one of the first writers to see how to build this insight into the human psyche into his plays. He created characters that expressed themselves poorly to others, and more importantly, to themselves, but with thrilling dramatic effect on the audience.

Acting students must learn to do something sophisticated and difficult when they face this kind of material, which is make the plot point clear by undercutting the dialogue and filling in with much behavior. To fail to do so in Chekhov is to render his plays meaningless.

The term *subtext* literally means that there is an essential plot point in the scene that is not directly expressed or referenced in the dialogue. Audience members must infer this point from the nonverbal behaviors of the actors, even at times when their words explicitly contradict the underlying point. Its originators used this term to describe a property of the text: a nonnegotiable element of the play itself. (*Subtext* isn't, as it is sometimes misused, simply a term for the inner life of the actor, but it is widely used as theatrical shorthand to convey the idea to students that acting consists of all kinds of nonverbal as well as verbal behaviors.) This dramatic technique, though new with Chekhov, became common in twentieth-century drama, and learning to play behaviors that revealed subtext became an essential acting skill. Stanislavski's insights into this literary phenomenon, and his work in training actors to deal with it, are probably the most influential part of his legacy.

Subtext is now a common part of theatrical vocabulary, and many young actors who have never heard of Stanislavski or Chekhov nonetheless know this term. Almost everything in modern acting training springs from the insight that an acting performance consists of far more than the words spoken in dialogue. Most of what follows in this book is aimed at building skills in the actor that were originally developed to deal with the demands of subtext.

A word of warning: Like almost any technique, creating an inner life can be overused. This arises because the skill has also proven useful in cases where there is no underlying plot point, but the text is minimal or banal (like, for example, much daytime television writing). Some actors are now used to "filling in" with interesting invention of their own on almost all occasions. When they get it wrong, creating a performance that misleads the audience about the text by adding layers of unnecessary and incomprehensible "subtext" of their own invention that is not in line with the play as written, it can be harmful. The early chapters of this book will help actors develop skills to create a full range of internal and external behaviors, and later (in Chapter 11) some guidance will be provided in aligning one's personal performance with the text to prevent misuse of the technique.

The Role of Instinct

We need not fear that we are devaluing or replacing instinct by seeking to understand it. Stanislavski certainly didn't. He sought to train his abilities so that he might preserve them. The whole point of the Stanislavski system is that instinct is good, that on occasion we can all act truthfully and artistically, but to be great artists we must be able to do so reliably *each time we perform*. His method is not an alternative to instinct, but a way of calling forth our natural abilities on cue. His system should not be thought of as a logical method that runs counter to what "natural" actors do. It is a way for actors to use their native abilities to the highest degree, every time they need them.

> *You want to see the difference between the art of representation and the art of lived experience?—go to the cinema. The audience is beginning to understand the difference and very soon will be demanding it from actors.*
> *—Stanislavski*

Stanislavski was sometimes ridiculed for his absolute devotion to the truth of human behavior. Many regarded the nuances of this acting style to be too small to be seen from the audience, given their distance from the stage. Stanislavski, however, held firm to his belief in the importance of really living the part. He brilliantly foresaw that the rising art form of cinema would transform audience perceptions.

In this, as in so many things, he proved correct. It was the successes of "Method" actors under the close scrutiny of film that finally cemented the reputation of his training methods and that in turn has called the stage to a higher standard. Stanislavski's observations are still valid. Great acting can still be described in Stanislavski's terms, and his goals are still our goals.

Controversy

Nonetheless, his system remains controversial and there is far from universal agreement about what constitutes his technique. This is largely because it does not exist in a single definitive form. Stanislavski did not leave a final unambiguous version of his system, nor did he think such a thing was possible. He saw his work as an ongoing process.

Stanislavski continued to experiment throughout his life. He would develop ideas, reject them, replace them, sometimes circle back to them. Many of his students became great master teachers themselves. Often they knew him for a relatively brief time (three or four of his thirty active years), and their work reflected Stanislavski's work at that point in his development.

> *The constant transformation in Stanislavski's thinking and methods were very often linked with his changing roles as an actor, director, writer, and teacher at the Moscow Art Theatre between 1897 and 1938.*
> —Mel Gordon

Stanislavski did write three books on the subject: *An Actor Prepares, Building a Character,* and *Creating a Role.* These books are required reading for every serious actor. On close examination, however, these writings are sometimes more confusing than revealing. "They are not in any sense how-to books," Mel Gordon correctly observes. Written in the style of a fictionalized novel tracing the training of a student and his group of friends, the books are able to be specific only when describing the theoretical mechanics of the system. Later on in this book, I discuss some of the advantages of this format and even adopt the technique myself, but for now let's just say that these works don't convert into step-by-step instructions.

Stanislavski wrote the books hurriedly and was displeased with the results. He felt the detail of the daily work was as important as the grand vision, but was disappointed that his books were unable to convey this technical detail. Unfortunately, a simple description of the externals of the studio work does little to explain it, and Stanislavski could only partially find the words to describe the inner state of the actor when he or she is working correctly. Most of the controversy surrounding Stanislavski-based training stems from disagreements among practitioners over how to fill in the gaps left in Stanislavski's descriptions of the practical day-to-day work.

The System in America

The Stanislavski system arrived in America prior to his writings, via some of his early students. They knew the work firsthand from their work in the studio. They taught the system just as they had learned it from Stanislavski or from his brilliant protégé, Evgeni Vakhtangov. They were, on the whole, unfamiliar with Stanislavski's grand vision, including his moral and ethical exhortations, which seemed to have played a very small part in his day-to-day teaching compared with their prominence in his writings and speeches. The exercises and experimentation that took place in the studio were the backbone of his school.

Several of America's most prominent acting teachers were pupils of Stanislavski's at one time or another. The founders of The American Laboratory Theater, Richard Boleslavsky and Maria Ouspenskaia, both remained behind when the Moscow Art Theatre toured America in 1924. Later Michael Chekhov, nephew of the playwright and Stanislavski's star pupil, came to America and taught. Some of the important teachers from the 1940s and 1950s, such as Lee Strasberg, Sanford Meisner, and Stella Adler, were pupils of these Stanislavski-trained greats.

Stanislavki's writings began to reach America in staggered and nonsequential order. They seemed to contradict some of what his earlier students were teaching. Apparently Stanislavski's work had continued to evolve: by the time he was ready to set down his system in writing, some aspects of it had changed. As a result, interpretations of Stanislavski's methods have taken many forms, and an equally good case can be made for the authenticity and validity of each. Controversy continues to rage around whether the early teachings were abandoned and repudiated as incorrect or merely set to one side once proven valid so the master could continue to research

Figure 2.3. Lee Strasberg was perhaps America's most famous acting teacher and an early promoter of Stanislavski's theories.

fresh ideas. Scholars of the writings tend to take the former view, inheritors of the practical work, the latter.

As might be guessed, the members of each group are highly influenced by the form in which they first encountered the system. Those that received the work from classroom instruction in exercises tend to stress the emotional elements of the work and are deeply in touch with the mystical aspects of Stanislavski's explorations. They are sometimes less tuned to the structural aspects of the grand vision. It is largely from this source that the "Method" acting associated with Lee Strasberg and the Actors Studio developed. This tendency still predominates in the independent studios in New York and Los Angeles.

Alternatively, those that know the work through Stanislavski's written legacy tend to stress its active, logical nature, deemphasizing aspects that do not have a clear niche in the system outline. This tendency predominates in American colleges and universities.

The fact that neither view is complete nor indisputably authentic should not blind us to the tremendous benefit each has given the profession. Stanislavski's concern with acting theory opened the way to serious explorations into teaching the art form and helped countless aspiring actors reach their goals of becoming trained, competent artists. Rather than bellicosely debate which view is the definitive Stanislavksi—a debate I believe unable to be resolved—I find it healthier to view the full spectrum of his legacy as fertile ground for exploration.

A major goal of this book is to use recent advances in other fields (especially brain research) to illuminate how and why the Stanislavski system works. Now is a very good time to return to Stanislavski's concern with the organic. Too little was known in his time to either confirm or repudiate his concept that a "natural" way of working existed. Now we can turn to more recent research that confirms many of his ideas. Along the way perhaps some light will be shed on the manner in which the two views of Stanislavski are really two sides of the same coin.

What Stanislavski Didn't Say

While we must respect the many different schools of thought about Stanislavski's teaching, there are a few ideas frequently associated with his name that should *not* be. The diversity of interpretation about his techniques and intentions has unfortunately left enough room for a few fraudulent impressions to gain wide acceptance. These mistaken beliefs are put forth by well-meaning but uninformed admirers as well as by detractors. Neither camp has ever taken the time to find out what Stanislavski did and didn't say. Be generous in looking at the many lines of thought about Stanislavski's work, but don't believe everything you hear with his name attached:

- Stanislavski didn't say, and didn't think, that good solid technical training was unimportant. His attempts to find ways to call forth intuition dependably were coupled with formal voice and body work; they didn't replace it. His own training program for students was extensive—dance, fencing, singing, voice, and deportment in addition to the work with which we are so familiar. Don't let anyone tell you that *all* you have to do is find your muse, or at least don't let them attribute such an opinion to Stanislavski.
- There is no indication anywhere that Stanislavski thought creating intense emotion through focusing on your personal life and history was the main point in acting. At most, Stanislavski encouraged his actors to be open to their own emotions. He occasionally helped his more repressed students empathize with their characters' situations by recalling the emotions that parallel experiences in their personal lives had evoked. He never indicated that this was to be used as a stage technique. The cultishness that has grown up around intense personal introspection is a great misunderstanding surrounding how and why Stanislavski (rarely) asked actors to think about what a play's given circumstance meant to them. Stanislavski did not favor emotional indulgence about either the past or the present. Nor should you.
- "Live the part," said Stanislavski, by which he meant experience it. More than a few people have misunderstood him to mean either that they should go out into the world playing their character in real situations, or that they should not bother to characterize the role at all. Each is an equally ludicrous interpretation. Stanislavski was telling actors to be sensorially alive and spontaneously aware. The context of his remarks always makes that clear. He believed that actors do

play roles, not substitute themselves for their characters, *and*
that they check the roles at the stage door on their way out
for the evening.

- There is occasionally a misunderstanding that because of all
the emphasis on internal process, Stanislavski did not care
about the audience. "Play well, or play badly, but always play
truthfully," can be understood to mean that if you are true to
yourself it doesn't matter what the audience thinks. If you
remember that Stanislavski was not just a theorist but a producer in one of the world's largest theatre companies, the mis-
informed nature of this assertion becomes clearer. Stanislavski
dedicated his life to his theatre company. He clearly cared
about audiences very much. An actor who ignored them or
shut them out didn't last long in his company.

3   The Brain as Stagehand

Throughout the last third of the twentieth century and particularly during the 1990s, enormous strides were made in neurocognitive studies, leading to a new understanding of how the human brain works. A scientific understanding of the mysterious and complex organ inside our head has opened new pathways in numerous fields, with acting studies being especially illuminated. Recent scientific study has helped us to see why the acting principles Stanislavski codified a century ago and subsequent teachers have continued to develop actually work. The insights afforded by this study are surprising. They have affirmed that many of the intuitive leaps that Stanislavski made were prescient, though the biological reasons that these principles work were not at all clear until very recently.

Because the brain controls everything we do and everything we understand about our world, cognitive study has, at least since the time of the ancient Greeks, been an important scientific discipline. But the operations of the brain are far too complex and minute to observe directly. Scientists have long had to resort to indirect supposition in understanding the functioning of the brain.

Until recently the main approach to understanding our mental processes was simply to think about how we think. Self-consciousness in the narrowest sense of that term was the primary tool for

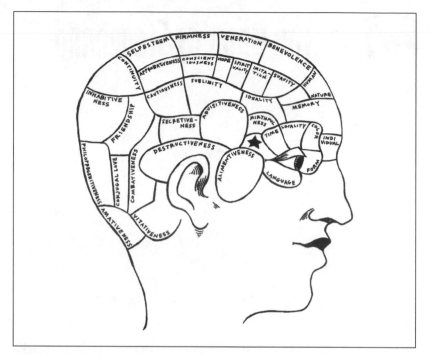

Figure 3.1. The brain as it was understood in the nineteenth century, with character traits assigned to specific areas. The acting style of the time, with stiff physical poses, correlates in interesting ways to the scientific theory underlying this drawing.

exploring the mental world. Unfortunately, thinking about our own thinking can be very misleading. A good deal of what was once believed to be proven scientifically has turned out to be wrong. For example, for years society and the scientific community have held that we use only a small portion ("10 percent" is the favorite figure) of our mental capacity. Now we know that is wildly incorrect. But the way in which we use our brain is much more sophisticated than even the most enlightened thinkers speculated a quarter of a century ago.

The Double Brain

The first steps toward a fuller understanding of how the brain functions were made in the Nobel prize–winning work spearheaded by Roger Sperry at the California Institute of Technology. Sperry and

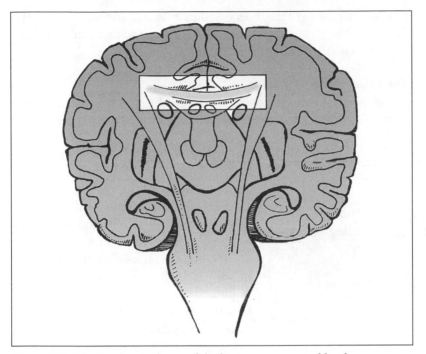

Figure 3.2. The two hemispheres of the brain are connected by the corpus collosum. *Severing this connection in severely epileptic patients opened our understanding of the functions of the left- and right-brain hemispheres*

his colleagues worked extensively with medical patients who suffered from severe epilepsy; a main aspect of treatment was to sever the connections between the two hemispheres of the brain.

These patients showed relatively few side effects from this procedure, which was medically very beneficial. But careful testing revealed that their brains now operated in ways aberrant to normal functioning. To greatly simplify, Sperry and his colleagues discovered that the two halves of the brain operate separately, and differently, from each other, almost as if they are two distinct brains.

The Dominant Hemisphere
The first great shock of their research was the discovery that almost all the mental functions considered by previous researchers and "thinkers about thinking" (things like use of language, analytical thought, and mental manipulation of numbers) occurred in only *one* of the two cortical hemispheres, usually the left. At first glance it

seemed that thought itself occurred in only half the brain. Believing this "thinking" hemisphere was much more advanced than the other, scientists named it the dominant hemisphere.

The Other Side of Things

The opposite hemisphere, usually the right, was named the minor hemisphere. Since its attributes were not immediately obvious, the researchers thought it to be a mute, immature reflection of the dominant hemisphere, undeveloped in any of the higher functions. Sperry's team began their work in earnest when they rejected the possibility that half the brain was undeveloped or redundant.

In 98 percent of right-handed people and 65 percent of left-handed people, the left hemisphere is dominant. For convenience's sake, the left hemisphere is therefore usually referred to as the dominant hemisphere.
—Betty Edwards

They discovered that the so-called minor hemisphere also specializes in the higher processing of information. However, rather than treat things sequentially, it synthesizes them: it creates multiple and simultaneous connections among bits of information. Unlike the dominant hemisphere, however, the minor hemisphere is not self-reflective. When operating independently, it does not have an awareness of working toward a solution. Because the "right brain" is not capable of language, it does not "talk" to us with the voice-in-the-head that characterizes dominant hemisphere thought. When the minor hemisphere processes information, we experience knowledge as a sudden flash of intuition, a feeling of "just knowing" the answer, even if we don't know how we got the answer. Thinkers about thinking were unaware of this part of the brain's workings, because they had never experienced its functions on the conscious level.

Sperry's team documented that the "minor" brain hemisphere is called into service anytime an extremely complex group of data has to be synthesized into a single complete understanding. An example is everyday freeway driving: we are keeping track of the progress of the cars that surround us, the speed of our own vehicle, our intended destination, the amount of time we have to get to our destination, our progress to date, the weather and driving conditions, and many other factors. Despite this flurry of data, we do it all with a sense of ease and comfort. Many people even report that driving is relaxing!

So the so-called minor hemisphere is not minor at all. It plays a major role in our lives. It is not an underdeveloped twin. It is not chaotic. It is involved in complex, higher-order mental functioning. It seeks out order and increases it. *Most important, it can be educated, just as the dominant hemisphere can, to do its job faster, with greater efficiency and to greater effect.*

What We Learned from Sperry

Sperry's work was the first indication that the brain "thinks" in more ways than the logical, linear manner of which we are self-aware. Sperry won the Nobel prize in medicine for far more than just articulating an understanding of brain structure. The implications of the work are enormous. It opened the door for new avenues into cognitive research and new understanding of our mental life. Sperry helped us understand that much of our thought takes place on previously unsuspected levels. Indeed, that thought is more complex than the direct experience of our own "thinking" can reveal. Science became fascinated by the full range of human thought, including the way it plays out in some activities—acting being one—that had previously lacked intellectual respectability. It also focused attention on more empirical (though of necessity still indirect) methods of exploring thought, the most revealing of which   artificial intelligence research—was just coming into its own.

In the two decades since Sperry received his Nobel prize, his findings about the so-called left-brain/right-brain phenomenon have been widely disseminated and highly influential. Unfortunately, they have also been vastly oversimplified. In trying to explain the phenomenon, some of its adherents have reduced the theory to mean only that the left brain is verbal, the right brain nonverbal. Though such a reduction contains a grain of truth, it overgeneralizes the idea, especially in the arts. In some quarters, a notion has sprung up that right-brain exercises are the answer to any problem—the kind of thing parodied by a graffito I once saw: "Left brains are evil, right brains are good!"

A Brief History of Artificial Intelligence

No field has proven so fertile for indirectly revealing *human* intelligence as that of *artificial* intelligence, the attempt to create "think-

In general, scientists have had a much easier time teaching a robot to perform the "higher" functions that formerly belonged solely to human beings (reading, proving theorems, diagnosing diseases) than the "lower" functions that animals have mastered (hearing, seeing, grasping objects). Improbably enough a robot is more easily taught to play expert chess than to move the pieces.
—Brad Leithauser

ing machines." This is ironic, in that artificial intelligence (AI) has to date failed to create anything like a truly intelligent machine, the reason being that what scientists thought they knew about the hierarchy of human thought has proved false. Tasks that seem elementary to us have turned out to be fiendishly difficult to program into a robotic machine. Other tasks that are almost impossible for a human have been programmed into a robot without difficulty.

Attempts to build an artificially intelligent machine date from the 1930s, the very dawn of the computer age. Even then, British logician Alan Turing (the subject of the recent play *Breaking the Code*) was envisioning a machine that went beyond mere calculation, and intelligently solved problems.

The metaphor underlying Turing's experiments, which were to set the direction of AI for decades, is a theory of mind that dates back as far as Plato. According to this theory, the brain gathers data, converts it into symbolic form, manipulates or combines the symbols, and generates a response; knowledge is the ability to apply a few fixed and universal rules to data gathered by the mind.

Retreating from Plato

Turing's experiments were not failures—far from it, since they resulted in the creation of computers—but their very success has forced a retreat from the theory that spawned them. The desktop computer is a nearly perfect Platonic machine, and it is nothing like the human mind. As anyone who has had a close encounter with a computer can tell you, though they may be powerful and effective at some tasks, they are not intelligent.

This paradoxical situation, where computers are millions of times better than humans at a few things but incorrectably bad at most things, forced a reevaluation of human intelligence. By building brilliantly successful logic machines, we discovered that the human brain isn't one.

It now seems cognitive researchers took the reports from "thinkers about thinking" too seriously for too long. Based on these reports scientists had decided the main human strategy for problem solving was step-by-step trial and error. But that is not the way the human mind really operates most of the time. We use the term *common sense* to describe the phenomenon of effortlessly and quickly applying vast amounts of worldly knowledge to a problem, including a great deal of emotional sorting, and reaching a solution without conscious processing. AI researchers didn't recognize how thoroughly common sense is intelligence. Formal logic is an exception to our usual processing, not the rule.

Over the course of fifty years, scientists realized that anything like real thinking was beyond the capabilities of machines using strictly rule-based symbolic manipulation, regardless of how much power or size was available. The human brain uses far more worldly methods of thought. The distinctions between "higher" forms of thought, such as reasoning and problem solving, and humbler sorts, such as seeing, using common sense, and remembering, are less solid than tradition would have it. Recent experiments in AI have found greater success in creating models of knowledge that treat the sensory and analytical frames of mind as equal partners.

> *The computer, the basis of artificial intelligence, has unmasked as comfortable delusions our long-standing ideas about the nature of human reason. In part these delusions arose, and lasted so long, because the worldly aspects of intelligence, the ones evolution spent so much time on, are buried so deep, are so much a part of our everyday being, we do not realize they exist. . . . Our access to the process of thinking, as opposed to its products, is severely limited. Often a verbal "explanation" of how we think is nothing but a plausible story.*
> —Jeremy Campbell

For the last four decades AI researchers have made serious attempts to give computers a sensory grounding, like the human brain has, but it has proven more difficult than the first attempters optimistically imagined. They had hoped to allow a computer to "see" by hooking it up to a video camera. That didn't work. The video camera, like the human eye, doesn't "see" at all, it merely gathers data about light. The act of perception happens in the brain. An artificial brain has to be programmed to attend to the data. Doing so turns out to be not a small background task but one of such enormous

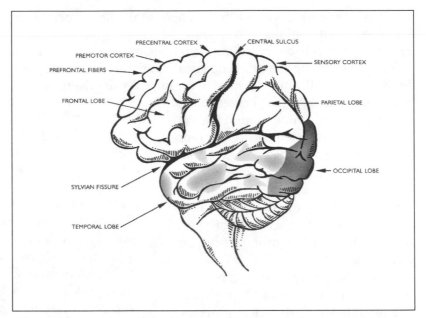

Figure 3.3. In contrast to the drawings of the nineteenth century, which concerned themselves with mapping the surface of the brain, the twenty-first-century model of the brain shows our increased fascination with its layers and structures.

complexity that at present it remains solvable only in small pieces. Working backward, neuroscientists were able to show that seeing (and other sensory processing) accounts for a huge amount of human mental energy. They began to understand where a large part of that "missing" 90 percent of brain potential was being used.

A New View of Thought

The intensely revealing work of artificial intelligence researchers and the insights of neuroscientists like Sperry have brought about a model of thought that rejects the old picture of detached, cold, empirical reasoning and replaces it with a more aware, emotional, worldly, and actively searching mind. The philosopher in the corner, a "thinker about thinking," has been replaced by an active, sensitive searcher who looks more like an actor every time new experimental data comes in.

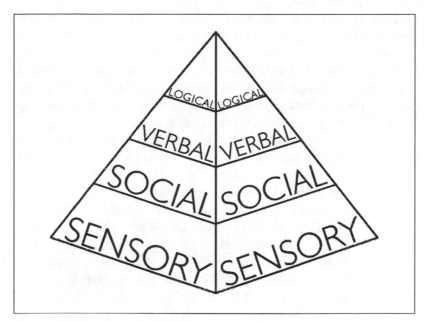

Figure 3.4. The pyramid of thought

This new model of thought is a series of layers, a pyramid (see Figure 3.4). At the bottom, larger than any other layer, is a foundation of sensory perception. The greatest portion of our mental resources is devoted to monitoring and observing our surroundings through our senses, and this huge stream of data is sorted and analyzed not by logic but by our emotions. The brain does most of this work unconsciously but nonetheless continuously. Without it we would forget to breathe, we would lose our balance and fall out of our chairs. Everyday life would be impossible. Take a second to observe people around you, and you will realize that they are almost constantly adjusting themselves, realigning their balance, pulling their coats about themselves for warmth, moving for better angles of sight, or turning their heads slightly to hear better. They are probably unaware of any of these small actions, but initiating and monitoring these movements consumes a remarkably large part of their mental energy.

Actors are much more aware of these things, because they start their performance process in a consciously self-created and entirely artificial environment. Stanislavski emphasized simple sensory awareness, which he called interacting with the "given circum-stances," because he recognized it as the bottom layer of human experience. Philosophers didn't observe this interaction with the world, because it had so little bearing on their private and secluded musings; Stanislavski saw it as the immense part of mental function-ing it is, because creating the world of the play from the ground up is such a large part of the performer's task.

The next layer of the pyramid, smaller than the first but still large, is social interaction. Much of our mental life, it seems, is spent monitoring and reacting to others. The rules of social behavior are remarkably complex. (Evolutionary biologists now theorize that a possible cause of man's enormous brain power was the complex stim-ulation provided by his early tribal origins.) Again, the philosophers often withdrew from social company to contemplate thought in iso-lation and didn't see social interaction as a vital part of mental life, an oversight impossible for the collaborative artist Stanislavski.

Above this level sits a third, still smaller layer, in which language comes into play. It is the layer at which we first become self-aware, so for many it is the first part of mental life noted. Though it is impor-tant, it plays a much smaller part in our mental life than cognitive science originally accorded it. Stanislavski was accurate here, too, although until evidence emerged to support his view, his critics often attacked him for undervaluing literature. (I believe this to be a misinterpretation of his teachings. He did *not* say that literature was unimportant, nor did he devalue it. He did, however, recognize it as a later concern in the actor's process than makes some scholars comfortable.)

At the very top of our pyramid sits a final layer, abstract thought. Compared with the layers that have preceded it, remarkably little mental energy is spent pursuing logical reasoning. Again, this is not to devalue such thinking, but only to note its relative weight.

What was wrong with previous cognitive theories was that they took a top-down approach, hypothesizing that the least common and most recently developed form of thought was a paradigm for the entire spectrum of human mental functioning. We now see thought as a bottom-up process, beginning in emotionally infused sensory awareness and interacting through a variety of layers. It is a richer and more rewarding view of intelligence.

Stanislavski's theories about acting, as well as more recent devel-opments in the field, are well in tune with this more complex and layered view of thought. Stanislavski concerned himself with total thinking as opposed to specialized abstract reasoning. Looking at the long line of "thinkers about thinking," we find they were usually philosopher/scientists examining their narrow and unworldly profession. Because of his special perspective, Stanislavski was better able to understand the total range of his thought processes.

> *Smell was our first sense, and it was so successful that in time the small lump of olfactory tissue atop the nerve cord grew into a brain. Our cerebral hemispheres were originally buds from our olfactory stalks. We think because we smelled.*
> —Diane Ackerman

Recent cognitive theorists, like Antonio Damasio and Richard Cytowic, have added to our understanding of the astounding complexity of thought at the foundational levels of our thought pyramid and the rich, multidirectional interactions of the layers. They have shown that even the most self-aware abstract logic is deeply infused with sensory and emotional processing simultaneously happening below the levels of conscious awareness. (Cytowic, in fact, has written a famous essay titled "Consciousness Is a Type of Emotion.")

The Feel of Total Thought

This book can be used in two ways: (1) to improve your acting by using information about how the entire spectrum of mental thought operates as a guide to sequencing your training or (2) as a guide to learning more about your mental potential by studying acting as a way of exploring total thought, including those parts that you can only indirectly induce.

Whichever approach you take, throughout it you'll be asked to return to the *feel* of the exercises, because creative thought induces a very different set of sensations than abstract analytical thought does. The latter functions by inhibiting much of your physical activity, literally shutting down parts of your brain with chemical messages. Words rise in your mind, and you become self-conscious in both good and bad senses of that term.

Sensory-based creative thought, by contrast, is liberating. It stimulates most parts of your brain into a simultaneous symphony of processing. It feels good, physically and emotionally, because you are not being physically inhibited or narrowly focused; you are using something much closer to your full potential. You feel relaxed. Because your awareness is outwardly directed, you feel a part of things instead of self-consciously separate. You feel confident.

This sense of well-being and wholeness is an important guide to your development. It is the "creative state" that Stanislavski describes, and as you've just seen, it is a neurological phenomenon. You really are thinking differently.

SOLO WORK

About the Exercises

There are literally hundreds of thousands of acting exercises that may be used in acting classes to teach actors new skills. These range from études in diction, verse speaking, and breath control to imagining oneself to be an inanimate object. Valuable as these are, they are of a different order from the exercises in this book.

The exercises here are designed to release capabilities *you already possess* but may not yet have connected to acting. They will help you learn to assume the frame of mind from which an actor works and to apply your thought processes to artistic performance. The exercises are purposely short, and each builds on the previous one. They are intended to show you the perceptual abilities innate in the brain and help you master these abilities. In a very fundamental way, they will teach you about your senses. At first you may be skeptical, feeling that you see, hear, taste, touch, and smell very well already. The exercises will teach you, however, that you can *consciously choose* to switch to a deeper, more perceptive way of sensing, which in turn results in richer and more truthful performances.

I have been teaching these exercises for several years, and my students have made remarkable and rapid progress. Most of them begin by giving very stilted and conventional performances, and most are plagued by some degree of stage fright. By concentrating on deeper, more perceptive ways of thinking, they are *almost to a person* able to free themselves from stereotypical acting ideas and thereafter give much more finely detailed and moving performances.

Of course, learning these ideas is not the end point of your study. You can spend a lifetime mastering all the nuances of the acting profession, including training your voice and body to express the ideas of the mind, studying great literature for the stage, and working as part of an ensemble. But the ability to sense clearly with the special perceptions of a creative artist is the necessary first step.

Getting Ready

The first condition of our work is to be willing to experiment. Acting is, for most, a different way of looking at things than we normally employ. It takes trust. Decide that you will not just read about the ideas in this book, but try them. Fear of failing or making fools of themselves prevents many aspiring actors from even attempting to learn the craft. Don't let fear stand in your way. You will occasionally fail at things you attempt in the theatre; there will be days when you look foolish. It's the price of trying things you've never done before. The theatre, however, is an accepting place. All of us who regularly work in it have been where you are. We, too, have tried things that didn't quite work and looked a bit foolish. Theatre, especially educational theatre, is built on an extension of trust among learners. We all know we need room to try things without having to be perfect the first time out. Make up your mind to be open to the possibilities. Trust that others undergoing the process with you will be understanding and supportive. Decide to be understanding and supportive in return.

A second condition, related but separate, is to develop theatrical discipline. Artists have a reputation for being indulgent and undependable. The reasons for this rumor are complicated, but it is not true. Participation in the profession requires an unwavering dedication. So many people want to be a part of this world that only the most dependable are considered for roles.

This is not to say that you must aspire to work professionally. This book is for anybody who wants to explore the operations of the mind. We can all benefit from the actor's discipline whether or not we intend to act professionally.

Make up your mind to be dependable in all your theatrical endeavors. Especially later, when you are working with a partner, be sure that you do what you say you will do. Attend rehearsals on time, carry out the solo work on the predetermined schedule, and generally carry your part of the load. Discipline will take you much farther than "talent" in learning your craft, and perhaps later in working in the theatre as well.

Finally, your work will be enhanced by starting from a point of relaxation. Before any work session, take a few minutes to set the cares and concerns of your life temporarily aside. Focus on your goal for the day, and forget the intrusions of the world for the length of your session. Back up this attitude with a brief physical routine to relax your muscles.

relaxation exercise

Lie on your back on the floor with your hands on the floor beside you. Starting with your feet, tense and release each part of your body.

Curl and stretch your toes as far as you can. Push them tensely toward the floor as far as you can. Then release them. Feel the sensation of relaxation.

Now point your toes back toward your head, tensing the feet as much as possible. Release. Tense and release the calves, the thighs, and the buttocks in turn.

Stretch your fingers out as far as they will go, tensing all your digits. Relax them. Tense and release your wrists, forearms, upper arms, and shoulders. Scrunch your neck down against your shoulders and then release it. Tense your face up, eyes clenched tightly. Purse your lips. Pull your face into a small little space as if you have just tasted the sourest lemon in the world. Now relax.

Feel in your body the sensation of tension and how good it feels to release the muscles afterward. Savor the relaxation.

Still lying on the floor, imagine the sensation of lying on the warm sand of a beautiful beach; let the heat melt all the knots out of your muscles. You haven't a care in the world. The weather is perfect and you are a limp rag, just lying there.

Now, with your muscles as relaxed as possible, flop one hand over onto your belly and just notice the automatic rise and fall of your breath. You needn't do anything about it, but just feel this little source of life and energy plugging away on its own while you rest.

Relaxation is not the same as sleepiness. Notice that you are mentally alert. Feel the breath as readiness for action. Your muscles have nothing to do now, so they have gone into neutral, but they are ready when called upon.

Now roll over onto your stomach and stretch like a cat waking up. Gently rise to your hands and knees and stretch backward and forward with the careful energy that felines bring to their waking ritual. Slowly stand up.

Savor the sensation of being completely relaxed and completely ready. Imagine that your head is a helium-filled balloon that rises up and away from your body on its own accord. (You are not pushing it up, it just floats there, impervious to gravity.)

Finish your ritual by shaking out your whole body, like a kid doing a crazy ants-in-the-pants dance. Look like a film of the hokey-pokey being fast-forwarded. Shake everything loose and then return to your calm neutral stance.

Congratulations, you are ready to work!

# 4   Concentration

The beginning point for mastering the kind of bottom-up thought characterized by Stanislavski's creative state is learning to concentrate. But how actors concentrate is not widely understood. Concentration is not a matter of thinking *harder*, but of thinking in a different way. In order to discover the potential of this kind of thinking, you need to experience it. Creative thought can be difficult to access, however, because of the habitual dominance of analytical thought patterns. One way to reach the creative state is to present your mind with a task for which your habitual, top-down (that is logical, sequential) response is not suited.

For the actor the first step toward learning to concentrate is not additive (learning to do something extra), but subtractive (learning to evade an old interfering habit). The kind of focused thinking we are after happens in a different part of the brain than habitual and cursory thought.

When operating from the top down, we are very good at supplying quick answers until we encounter tasks that are too complex for a rapid symbolic understanding. Whenever data is complicated, unfamiliar, or difficult to categorize, our logical mind declines to process it. It will also decline problems that are too detailed and/or repetitive. If we were to personify our top-down operating mode, we would say it is impatient. To bypass it, we must present it with a task it finds boring or difficult.

To experience bottom-up thinking—the creative state—we need to return to our sensory base. We need to *feel* what it's like to undergo the cognitive shift.

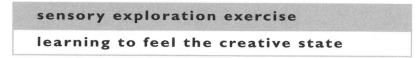

sensory exploration exercise

learning to feel the creative state

This exercise takes about twenty minutes. Set an alarm or ask someone else to keep track of the time. Timekeeping is a logical function that interferes with the switch to sensory thinking.

1. Choose a simple object that stimulates several of the senses. A soft drink in a can, for example, has a specific texture (smooth and metallic), temperature (cool), feel (slightly malleable), smell (of the drink), taste (both the metallic "tang" of the can when licked and the drink inside), sound (when opened or struck with the fingers), and distinctive look (the packaging). Other possibilities are cosmetics, snack foods, beverages, or cooking utensils.
2. Sit in a comfortable chair with your hands resting in your lap, the object in your hands. Don't use a desk or table. Begin to shift the object around slightly and note the various sensations you are experiencing. Examine the object millimeter by millimeter. Identify the one sensation that is most pronounced at the moment.
3. Paying no attention to the way you would normally treat the object, see if you can find a way to maximize the sensation. For example, you might touch the soft drink can to your face to really gauge its temperature.
4. While doing this, do your best to avoid naming or describing the sensation. Labeling is a logical function. Concentrate instead on the location (where on your body you are receiving it) and intensity of the sensation. For example, concentrate on the slight pressure on your fingertips caused by the weight of the can as you hold it. You may need to treat the

object in unconventional ways to find the maximum sensation: don't be bound by your usual relationship to it.

5. Once you are convinced you are experiencing the sensation as strongly as possible, slowly repeat several times the step that brought you into strongest contact. For example, touch the can to your face for a few seconds, remove it, then after a few seconds touch the can to your face again. Observe carefully the physical reception of the sensation.

6. Set the object aside. Note, now, what is *physically memorable* about your exploration. By loosely reenacting the repeated step you will be able to re-create the memory of that particular sensation without manipulating the object, because you have memorized the sensory details. Play with this a few times, perhaps handling the object again if your memory starts to fade.

7. Move on to the second strongest sensation of the object and repeat the steps. Then go on to the third strongest and so on until you can sensorially re-create the entire object or until the alarm sounds.

Do the exercise now, before reading on. After you have finished, evaluate your experience.

The most common mistake in executing this exercise is rushing. In order to shift to the new mode, the brain has to be either bored or fed a great deal of complex information. Take the time to concentrate on the smallest details rather than rushing to a big conclusion.

Typically, you will feel mentally conflicted in this exercise. Many students report a verbal battle going on inside their head. They find themselves thinking and saying things like *This is stupid, This has no purpose,* and *This is boring.* Don't be concerned if this was your initial response. This self-talk is a manifestation of internal chemical inhibitors suppressing the processing shift to another area of the brain. You literally have to wait it out, which generally takes between thirty and ninety seconds.

Remember how different you felt once the shift occurred? At this point, you began to see how beneficial creative processing can be. By the end, your attention was solely on your perception of the object; earlier distractions had faded away. Creative processing increases concentration and eliminates self-consciousness because it lacks a "reporting voice."

It is common to experience a daydreamlike state with no awareness of the passage of time, a sense of peace and calmness. Creative processing, by eliminating critical self-consciousness, increases physical and mental relaxation.

You may also have noticed a reduced objectivity (no sense of watching yourself) as you became engrossed in the process. This experience is the basis for experiencing your character in the first person (*I am doing this*) instead of the third person (*Hamlet would do this*), a point we will have more to say about later.

A few people (and many others confirm the sensation when it is brought to their attention) say they feel released during this exercise by really noticing the object for the first time, even though they handle it almost every day. Some use the object in wildly imaginative ways, almost like a child playing. This, too, is a benefit of creativity. Creativity is the route to what we commonly call the subconscious. One of the basic goals of the Stanislavski system is to find a way to use "conscious technique to reach the unconscious." Let's reword that goal to clarify how creative thought is the key to this ability: *We want to use our conscious technique to shift to a mode that makes all sorts of mental connections (the creative state), including connections to our subconscious side.*

If you repeat this exercise enough times, you will notice a tendency to gravitate to the same sense over and over. It is normal to have a decided preference for one of your senses and to find it more highly developed and discriminating than the others. Most everyone prefers one of the three dominant senses: sight (visual), sound (auditory), or touch (kinesthetic). Taste and smell are interesting and powerful, but they are rarely dominant.

Whatever your preference, it doesn't affect your ability to act. You are learning to work sensorially as opposed to analytically. Frequent repetitions of this exercise will help train and improve your subdominant senses until they are as strong as those you prefer.

While doing this creative work, you may experience a feeling some people describe as *spacey* or *floating*. It is a different state. The usual first sign is a dropping away of the conscious "voice" you hear while labeling and ordering things. A lost sense of time or a great lessening of urgency is typical. There is no longer a feeling of logical order, but instead a feeling of intense concentration on the

Figure 4.1. In the creative state, actors become absorbed in intense concentration while physically relaxing the body.

object. For most people, this combination of effects is very pleasurable. In fact, in trying to re-create this state, the single strongest guide is a generalized feeling of well-being.

Occasionally people draw a blank on the experience. The usual tendency to use logic for problem solving can be so strong that the sensations of creative thought are unrecognized. These people react with phrases like *I wasn't really doing anything* or *It didn't feel any special way.* They are almost unaware that work occurred. Do not be concerned if you are one of them. Eventually these new sensations will become familiar and recognizable, but they need time to register in the mind. Someone with this initial reaction will, over time, benefit from this exercise more than anyone else.

The object of the sensory exploration exercise is to strengthen awareness of the shift to another mode of thought. It can

> *If I had to answer the question, What is the most important ability for the actor? ... the answer would emphatically be listening. Lest there be some misunderstanding, let me define what I mean by listening. I am talking about listening with all the senses.*
> *—Tony Barr*

serve you throughout your life and career by helping you access your creative side in almost any situation. *To be most effective, actors always want to perform in the rich sensorial mode we call the creative state.* The reductive nature of logic is not detailed or dynamic enough to hold the stage.

To summarize, the creative state can help actors:

- Increase concentration.
- Increase physical and mental relaxation.
- Reduce self-consciousness.
- Tap the subconscious.

These are many of the aims of the Stanislavski system.

Student Portraits

Lynne

For her sensory exploration, Lynne has chosen a can of her favorite cola. She seems dubious about the exercise, but is willing to give it a shot just to see what will happen. She confesses, however, that she chose the cola as her object because she expects the caffeine will get her through the anticipated boredom.

> It is ironic that the way to achieve focus is not through trying to exclude inappropriate thoughts and sensations, but by achieving greater responsiveness to appropriate ones.
> —Richard Hornby

Like most others in the group, Lynne is slow to settle into the exercise. She is particularly bothered by the prohibition against talking and mutters amiably to a nearby friend until her instructor asks her specifically to be quiet.

Once she begins her work in earnest, she is rushing. She is examining the can visually but turns it too rapidly in her hands. The instructor quietly asks her to slow the process *way down*. "Examine the can literally inch by inch," he says. Still it is a few seconds before she does so. Slowly, though, she is overtaken. Her gaze becomes very fixed. Her random movement quiets. She is suddenly very intense. She is completely unaware of her surroundings, focused solely on her task. She looks relaxed but very intense.

For the rest of the time, she never glances away from her job.

The silence in the room is profound. When the instructor announces that time is up, Lynne appears almost shocked. She shakes her head as if she had been suddenly caught daydreaming. When her instructor asks for discussion, Lynne volunteers that she learned things about her favorite drink in that twenty minutes that she had never noticed in years of drinking one or two cans a day.

"What did you learn?" the instructor asks.

"It tastes terrible."

The other students laugh, and the instructor asks if she is really telling them that she has discovered that she doesn't like the taste of her favorite drink.

Yes, she says, that is it exactly. Once she savored the liquid very slowly, she realized that the carbonation burned her mouth and had a bitter aftertaste that disturbed her. She says she could feel it peeling the enamel off her teeth. She now sees that she had never really paid any attention at all to her drink; she was surprised to find so much about it that was new once she really focused on it in detail.

Others in the class report similar experiences. Few of their discoveries are as dramatic as Lynne's, but most agree they never anticipated finding anything about the object to notice after the first minute or so; nevertheless, once they began they found that the twenty minutes flew by and were filled with discovery.

Sam

Sam is so skeptical that he has not even bothered to bring an object to the session. He is certain that he already notices everything, so the exercise will be a big waste of his time.

Often nothing comes when students don't even want to try. But Sam's instructor has an idea. He tells Sam to pick one sensory stimulus, a specific color, and spend the entire time seeing how widespread it is in the immediate environment. "Look around and notice everything in this room that is red."

Like Lynne, Sam becomes very focused about two or three minutes into the exercise. When the exercise is finished, Sam has a totally new attitude. He indicates that he certainly saw things with a clarity he had never previously experienced. "It wasn't just that there was more red than I anticipated, but that some of the things that were red, I had never noticed at all—like the fire alarm switch, exit signs over the doors, the ruby ring that Larry is wearing."

Still, it is not the immediate perceptual results of the exercise that most impress Sam. He is genuinely surprised to find that he has been in an identifiable alternate state. He describes the feelings he had while performing the exercise. He was aware of a great sense of relaxation coming over him. He completely lost track of time, of the sense that time was passing. He felt like he was in a science-fiction movie, where everything was frozen except him. "I did not want it to end. I was angry when you said time was up. You disturbed one of the most interesting things that has ever happened to me." Using a metaphor based on location, he says he "did not want to come back."

Sam's reaction touches off a long discussion. Most of the group members have felt this perceptual shift and are surprised by it. Some ask what the trick behind it is. There is no trick, however. We are always capable of attending to the information being gathered by our senses, but most of us are just too busy or preoccupied to do so.

A couple of the students focus on the part of the exercise where they reexperienced the sensation without the object. Tom says, "Once I put the glass down and then *faked it* [this phrase immediately catches the instructor's ear] I could still actually feel it. I could drink out of it just like the real thing. How can that be?"

Of course, it is not *just* like the real object, but Sarah has a good analogy: "It's like when I remember my favorite song. I know it is not coming from anywhere but inside me, but still I can *hear* it, in a way."

Which leads to the next topic.

> *Seeing, as we think of it, doesn't happen in the eyes but in the brain. In one way, to see flamboyantly, in detail, we don't need eyes at all. We often remember scenes from days or even years earlier, viewing them in our mind's eye, and can even picture completely imaginary events if we wish.*
> —*Diane Ackerman*

The Reality of Imagination

The most important result of working with the senses is that it creates a kind of grounding for your perceptions, which in turn anchor your acting. Because you are dealing with sensation instead of symbols, your mind responds by telling you that your perceptions are solid rather than abstract.

This solid sense of reality is peculiar because it can exist in response to stimuli created by the imagination. Apparently the

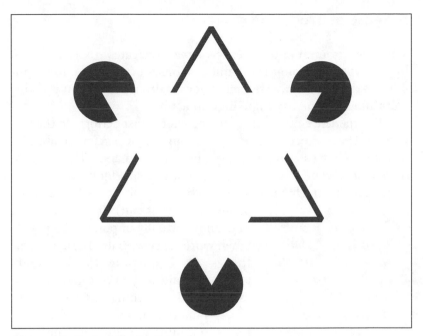

Figure 4.2. Optical illusion triangle

mind decides what is real based on the perceptual mode it has used to explore it. Things processed through the senses (bottom-up thinking) register differently from things pondered as abstractions (top-down thinking). The almost physical reality of an illusion is demonstrated in Figure 4.2. You not only *interpret* the triangle lying over the partially outlined triangle, you *see* it. It has a distinct edge, even in the areas where there isn't one. As with most optical illusions, even after you know the principle behind it, you still cannot change its effect.

You can induce this phenomenon for yourself. Imagine for a moment that you have a wedge of lemon in your hand. Remember what it is like to hold one between your thumb and forefinger. After a few seconds move the wedge to your mouth and take a big bite. Suck on the imaginary lemon. You will find that you salivate to dilute the anticipated acidity of the lemon, even though you know it exists only in your imagination. Your imagination interacts with your physical systems in much the same way that reality would.

A Sense of Truth

This firm grounding in a sense of reality creates *a sense of truth* because it stems from the organic responses of the mind, functioning as it does in the rawest circumstances, from the bottom up. This truthfulness is the key ingredient in acting.

To experience this sense of truth, actors must perform in the first person. They "experience" events through their perceptual abilities instead of giving a generalized, symbolic performance. This is a fundamental precept of realistic acting. Stanislavski enjoined his actors to refer to their characters in the first person at all times (*I am doing this, I want that*). It is a good rule of thumb, virtually impossible to violate when working sensorially. In such a case things *are* happening to you. Only abstracting allows you to think of them as happening to "your character."

> Part of keeping an actor independent is teaching him to know the difference between the lie and the truth of his work, to feel the difference. I think sense memory work is the way to teach that.
> —Dale Moffit

An important note: "A sense of truth" refers to finding the truth of your physical actions and perceptual reactions. Actors do not believe that they *are* their characters. To think you are Hamlet rather than yourself is clearly insane. Rather, you think, *If I were in Hamlet's situation this is how it would feel to me*. Stanislavski called this shift in thinking the "magic if."

A New Perspective

The sensory exploration exercise "turns off" your habitual top-down thinking because it is too full of sensory information and proceeds at too slow a pace for logic to handle successfully. Logic defers to your creative side, which is more suited to the job. It is an example of the way we normally use creativity in life: to address that which is rich, complex, and too difficult for by-the-numbers solutions.

We can keep from falling into our old habits by making a task intentionally difficult. Our logical mind is not very good at recognizing even familiar objects and ideas when they are presented in an unusual way. Turning a drawing upside down, for example, makes it harder to recognize what it is a drawing of. The following exercise sets up conditions unfavorable to your logical mind so that you can better tap into your creative side. You may be surprised by the result.

logic exercise
the artist at work

Gather two or three sheets of plain white paper and a pencil. *Read all the instructions before you begin.*

1. At the end of this chapter is an ordinary line drawing that has been printed upside down. When you look at it, it may not be immediately clear what it is.
2. *Without turning it right side up,* copy the drawing. Begin at the top of the page and work by estimating lines, curves, and angles. When you come to parts that you recognize, avoid naming them; continue to view them only as lines.
3. Work through the entire picture as if you were putting together a jigsaw puzzle, one odd-shaped piece at a time.

Do the exercise now, before reading further. After you have finished, evaluate the experience.

Turn both your completed drawing and the printed drawing right side up to look at them. The quality of the copying is usually surprisingly good—much better than if you had tried to copy the drawing in its right-side-up position. The accuracy of detail on top of detail creates the picture, not the knowledge of what is being symbolized.

Betty Edwards designed this exercise to help visual artists recognize that sensory-based creative thought is far better equipped to handle the complex operations of visual decision making. Logic, which is appropriate for giving quick, easy labels or creating simple symbols, is not able to handle the sensory discrimination required by these complex tasks. Logic is not as necessary as most people think. Purely sensorially you produced a reasonable copy of the line drawing, even though you may not logically have identified it.

Student Portrait

Eric

Eric's experience with this exercise is pretty standard, but he is quite articulate in analyzing his drawing. His first response, seconds after turning the drawings over, is that his is very bad. He roundly denounces it after a cursory glance and within fifteen seconds has turned it face down. As the drawing instructor who has come to class for the day begins to point out the peculiarity of the original, however, Eric becomes intrigued. He turns his own drawing back over and notices that many of the qualities he disliked in his drawing are copied from the original drawing. It is oddly proportioned and is not always put together logically. The chair in the drawing, for example, is actually a group of lines that give an illusion but do not add up to a literal depiction.

Soon Eric realizes that he has copied the picture reasonably well. He is surprised that his drawing in fact makes sense. He notes that he rejected his work immediately, before he really looked at it. Several of his classmates respond that their drawings really *are* bad, and Eric begins wandering about the room, showing each of them that his or her work is really much better than supposed. Eric's quick turnaround is fascinating, and the instructor gives him free rein: he is doing what that instructor had planned to do but doing it much more convincingly.

Even after Eric convinces them, several students wonder aloud how it can be that they drew so well, and assume it to be a fluke or a trick. But Eric understands exactly what has happened. "None of us could have drawn it well if it had been right side up, because we would have drawn what we *thought* we should see. We got it right because we were forced to rely on our senses instead of just half doing it and half filling in from some idea we had in our heads about how it should look." Eric has had an epiphany: he routinely lets old stereotypes interfere with his own abilities. This day marks a great turning point for him. He has a renewed faith in abilities that had been dormant and below the surface.

Trusting Creativity

It seems odd that we are able to copy a drawing better when it is upside down and difficult to identify than when it is right side up, but such is the paradox of our logical, analytical mind. With no symbols in mind, unsure of the subject of our drawing, we can still reproduce it with great precision.

We tend to think that the more information we have—the more logical our assessment of a situation—the better we will perform. There are certainly situations in which this is true, but other situations operate under different rules. Our ability to draw, for example, is liberated when we free ourselves from the tyranny of logical overanalysis. Without our usual symbolic knowledge to depend on, we see what is actually there. We are seduced into *a different way of thinking,* a way appropriate for the task at hand.

For now, all we need to extract from this experience is that we can *trust* our creativity. We are competent in ways we did not realize. Sometimes, even without our usual sense of being in control, we can produce high-quality results.

Let's Review

Before going on to theatrical applications, it might be helpful to go back and review your experiences with "shifting gears." You have now done so twice, during sensory exploration and upside-down drawing. Remember how creative processing *felt* different from logical work.

When operating creatively you were deeply absorbed in your task. You concentrated on the detail in front of you. That concentration blocked out an awareness of the passage of time. You were indifferent to how long the task was taking. You were unaware of what was happening outside the task. You probably were not talking to yourself, not even silently, and fought off any outside noise as a distraction.

Remember the sense of well-being. Creative processing (or the absence of logical processing) created a sense of pleasant relaxation. You felt at one with your work.

Journal Entry: Your Creative States

To round out your work on this set of exercises, return to the journal you began in Chapter 1. Make a new entry under the heading

Alternate Perceptual Modes. List the times and places you are aware of shifting into a different mode of thought. When do you slide off into this state? You have had two chances now to *feel* the shift, and you may recognize the sensation as familiar. Is this a state you enter with any frequency? Are there certain activities that trigger it in you?

Over the next few days, notice your changing perceptual modes. Keep careful notes about them. Don't be surprised if you find, more often than not, that the creative state slips up on you rather than being consciously induced. When this happens, write down what you were doing and see if you can deduce what conditions led to the switch.

Each time you repeat a sensory exploration exercise or do an additional drawing exercise, enter a few notes about your observations and discoveries.

Related Optional Exercises

Relaxation
1. Sit on the floor. With the knuckles of one hand, knead the bottom of the opposite foot under the arch, digging in slightly to loosen chronically tight muscles. Switch feet. With both hands, massage the tops of the feet. Using just your hands, with no help from the muscles in the ankles, pivot and loosen the ankles. Massage up the calves of the leg, stimulating the circulation. Move up to the thighs. With your hand like a large claw, gently pinch and loosen the muscles over the hip. Tip up onto one side and massage the opposite buttock. Switch sides. Use one hand to gently pull the fingers of the other hand, lengthening and loosening them. Switch hands. Shake both hands free at the wrists. Use one hand to massage the muscles of the opposite forearm and then the upper arm. Pinch and loosen the muscles of the shoulder. Switch hands and do the other side. With both hands, massage the muscles of the neck, starting at the shoulders and working up to the base of the skull. With the heels of the hands, make long downward strokes over the jaw. Start at the base of the ears and stroke downwards until your hands meet under the chin. Use your fingertips to massage your cheeks, nose, and forehead. Finish by massaging the scalp gently. Lie there on the floor and enjoy the sensation of muscular freedom.

2. Sit in a chair and determine what is the least amount of energy you can use to maintain your seated position. Pare back to the essential. Now, starting with your right foot, individually tense each muscle on the right side of your body, working from bottom to top. Try to keep the left side totally relaxed for comparison. Again, slowly working muscle by muscle, relax all the tensed muscles on the right side. Now try the same on the left. Monitor to see if you can tense each individual muscle without affecting those around it, or on the other side of the body. Feel and enjoy the release of each muscle.

3. Imagine that each muscle in your body is mystically attached to a concern in your life that is causing that muscle to tense. Visualize setting aside the care that is pulling on, stretching, and tensing the muscle. As you set aside the care, breathe deeply and release the muscle as if it were coming out from under a burden. Allow the muscles to enjoy their new freedom by stretching and yawning. Use your imagination to pretend that your muscles are just awakening from a long dormancy caused by the parasitic cares. Let them wake up and celebrate.

Concentration

1. Set a timer for fifteen minutes, or ask someone to keep track of the time for you. During this time put your attention on one stimulus only. For example, look for everything in your immediate surroundings that is colored blue. Look for as many examples of this color as you can find. Put your full attention into sensing this color in even the most minute quantities or in obscure places. Attend only to the sensation of blue. Or listen for a specific note. Play a tone on the piano, and listen to all the sounds in the environment to see if they match this pitch. Or check, through touch, the temperature of items in your environment. See if you can match things with the same surface temperature. In all cases, keep your attention solely on the sensations. Perform the exercise slowly and methodically, so that your top-down, logic-driven mode becomes bored and you enter the creative state.

2. Set a timer for twenty minutes. Using only your memory, try to reconstruct for yourself (in precise detail) a specific part of your day. Think of everything you did, every item you ate, every word you spoke. See it all as a movie in your mind. Go

so slowly that the time taken to reconstruct the activities is the same as it took to do them in the first place. Afterward recall the point at which you no longer had to fight for concentration, when the exercise took over. Repeat the exercise with distractions in the room. Turn on the television or the radio. Pay no attention to them, but keep your mind on the sensations of the day.

3. Look at the room you are in, all of it. Examine it in detail. Now close your eyes and re-create every detail in your mind. Create the most vivid pictures that you can, then open your eyes to see how well you did. Repeat this until the picture in your mind is as clear as the room itself.

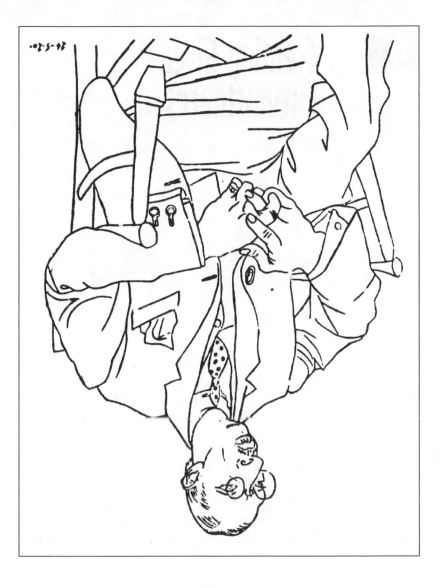

Creating Given Circumstances

Nearly a century ago, the great actress Eleanora Duse became an international star for the phenomenal performances she gave throughout Europe. Perhaps the most remarkable aspect of this career was that she achieved fame and critical acclaim performing in her native language, Italian, even though that was rarely the language spoken by her audience. So vivid was her acting that she overcame the barriers presented by performing in a language foreign to those watching her.

Duse's art transcended the formal rhetorical style popular in her time. Audiences were not disturbed that they could not understand the lines she spoke. Her acting was so expressive and truthful that they could follow the story because they understood the situation. Her ability was not that of a great "speaker," but that of one who could convincingly create the details of the world so fully and realistically that words became unnecessary.

Duse was, of course, one of the greatest actors who ever lived, but the principle that guided her acting is one we can all learn and apply. It is a simple extension of an idea we noted first in Chapter 3: *in the structure of human thought sensation is more fundamental than, and precedes, abstraction.* In other words, the rich, sensory thinking of the creative state comes before logic. For the actor in performance, it means that you think very little about your "character" but, instead, concentrate fully on your situation.

This is not just a theoretical idea about an approach to acting; it's the way people act in their everyday lives. You do not walk around every day saying, *I am a good and moral person, but I feel a bit melancholy,* or, *I must be happy and trustworthy.* We do not think about showing our own "character" to other people. Instead, our conscious thought focuses on the world around us: *Here comes my friend James. It's warm out here. I'm getting hungry.* In life, we automatically concentrate on the sensory context of our world. We do it so naturally that most of the time we are unaware it is happening.

This perfectly natural life process does not come naturally on stage, however, because the stage is not like life. It is not a natural environment, but an imaginary one. Knowing that the environment is artificial, we habitually apply to it the abstract thought process we use to cope with unnatural situations. We think logically about it.

> *Complex forms of thought go on below the level of awareness, so that conscious deliberation may be only a tiny part of intelligence, and perhaps the least interesting part; the tip of a huge iceberg whose existence we overlook because we have almost no insight into the hidden machinery of thought.*
> —*Jeremy Campbell*

We have looked thus far at the abilities we have at our disposal. Now we will begin to look at how we can *use* those abilities to override the tendencies forced on us by the unnaturalness of the stage. We can learn to behave there much closer to the way we do in life, but to do so we have to break our old habits of treating a script as a set of speeches and begin to see it as the blueprint for an entire world.

The key is to create layered thought from the ground up, beginning with a sensory concentration on the physical details of our environment. In life, this process is automatic and usually transpires on a level completely unnoticed by our conscious mind. While acting, we will have to play a more active role in creating this fundamental layer of thought.

The technical theatre term used to describe all the details that make up the situation is *the given circumstances.* It refers to all the conditions placed on the actor by the playwright and augmented by the director: the imaginary time and place in which the play is happening; the weather and other environmental conditions; the relationships between the characters; even the physical and emotional nature of our character.

The actor's first job is to identify the given circumstances. It is not enough to note them, however. That is merely abstraction. The danger lies in producing a set of symbolic actions to demonstrate a logical understanding of the text, as opposed to living it. An actor must create them sensorially, in the manner applied in the sensory exploration exercise.

---

given circumstances exercise

an everyday task

Using no props, physically re-create an everyday task such as making and drinking a cup of instant coffee or washing dishes. Any routine activity will do. Perform the exercise silently. Don't simply go through the steps or try to get the appearance right. This is not a performance for others. Re-create the *sensations* of the task for yourself. Concentrate on remembering how it *feels* to do a task, not how you think it should look.

Do the exercise now, before reading on.

The principle behind this simple exercise is precisely the same as that behind sensory exploration, except the actor is not just passively sensing but actively doing. It was one of the first exercises taught in America by the practitioners of the Stanislavski system. Richard Boleslavsky, one of Stanislavski's pupils, used it in his studio after he moved to New York.

Stanislavski rightly noted that the application of this exercise to theatre art is direct. First, it teaches the frame of mind from which actors do all their work (sensorial and spontaneous rather than symbolic/analytic and preplanned). Second, it helps actors learn to work by feel rather than by concentrating on appearances. Finally, it helps actors notice and observe their lives. The simple act of re-creating an everyday task, sensation by sensation, promotes an awareness of detail.

My students usually find this exercise very enjoyable. It is simple and relaxing. Some use it as a warm-up exercise to concentrate their minds before a performance. It can quickly induce the creative state desired by the actor. Best of all, there is a never-ending supply of material. We never run out of everyday tasks.

Student Portraits

Lisa

A graduate of a high school of the performing arts, Lisa has more acting experience than anyone in the class, but she is having difficulty grasping this exercise. Her previous training is obviously getting in her way, as she keeps reverting to "mime." Her task, making her bed, is clearly recognizable from her actions, but they look anything but natural. She keeps establishing the size and shape of the bed with stylized mime gestures. Her instructor interrupts, asking her to recall how it really *feels* to make her bed: "When you are all alone in your room, making your bed, do you begin by walking all around the perimeter and feeling its edges?" he asks.

Lisa says that of course she doesn't, but if she didn't do that here the group wouldn't understand what she was doing.

Her instructor explains that this is not the point of the exercise. He just wants her to re-create the actual sensations of the task. Her friends don't have to be able to guess what she is trying to *show* them.

"Then what is the point?" Lisa asks. She does not immediately see that she can do something on a stage for her own benefit. As long as she is standing on a stage she feels obligated to give her audience something, even if it is a stereotypical image.

It takes a good deal of convincing, but she agrees to try re-creating the sensations without being concerned about the audience. When she does, she is instantly more relaxed—and, surprisingly, also much more detailed—than when she was worrying about including defining details. The group is supportive. She is not only more interesting this way but also a much better performer, even measured by her own standards. Because her concentration is more focused, she is less self-conscious and less stereotypical.

That she is better when she is not trying to be a performer is a paradox Lisa is not quite ready to accept, however. The group has glimpsed an important principle, but Lisa will not believe it until she observes someone else doing the exercise.

Dan

Dan works for a retail clothing store. One of his daily jobs is to refold merchandise that has been tried on or handled by customers and restock it on the shelves. He has decided to use this activity for his exercise because he realizes that he does it by "feel."

For Dan this exercise is so simple he can scarcely see the point. He takes only a second or two to decide how he will map the basic geography of his workspace over the performance space, and then executes his exercise. He is so intent on his task that he does not introduce or explain it, he just begins.

The instructor is impressed by his work, but Dan does not see that he has really done anything. The other class members, however, do. They were given no clues about the exercise whatsoever, yet it was very clear to all of them what was happening, where it was happening, even at what time of day. They are amazed at the amount of detail that Dan was able to include.

Dan just laughs. He says that he made no attempt to include these extra details, and never thought about them while doing the exercise. The students, he says, are reading too much into his simple exercise. But they persist. "The cash registers are to your left, aren't they?" asks one. Dan reiterates that he did not include the cash registers in his exercise. "But that is where they are, isn't it?" Well, yes, Dan concedes. Another person identifies where the clock is kept in the store. Dan insists that he didn't think about the clock while doing his exercise, but several individuals distinctly remember him glancing at it. They turn out to be correct about the location.

The discussion continues for almost half an hour. Dan realizes that he was only concentrating on a few sensory details, the broadest outlines of his experience, but he unconsciously included much more. His friends realize that these unconscious additions are an important part of what Dan accomplished, that they are representative of our powers of sensory recall.

Concentrating on Sensation

The everyday-task exercise can feel easy, some would say too easy. Don't worry if it is not an effort to do this exercise. You're using your imagination, not calculating cube roots.

Alternatively, sometimes it takes a few attempts before you can really concentrate on remembering exactly *how it felt* to do a task. Old habits are difficult to discard. It is not uncommon for the first try or two to be a mime exercise in which the performer tries to signal a viewer by concentrating on a few symbolic gestures that convey the essence of the action. Concentrating on physical sensation will soon free you from this artificial style. The results are clear to an observer, but it is the actor herself who will really understand the difference. There is a tangible freedom that comes from concentrating on sensation instead of appearance.

This exercise is deceptively simple. It is not difficult to do well, but it is about more than it seems on the surface. It is a way of working that is more rewarding than it initially appears. Only by watching your colleagues work do you really see what they have done.

> *Human memory cannot help but connect one thing it knows to another thing it knows. It puts the world together in such a way that, given a small fragment of information, it can amplify the fragment instantly into a sizable parcel of knowledge.*
> —*Jeremy Campbell*

Starting Small

One of Stanislavski's most useful observations is that creativity always starts small. Remember that when drawing the upside-down figure, you didn't need to understand it; you just needed to focus on one small corner and begin. And in sensory exploration, the area of sensory awareness that triggers the re-creation is actually very small. The pressure on the thumb, for example, may be the specific sensation that helps you to "feel" the cup holding your soft drink.

Regardless of what you are asked to create, this principle will hold. An imaginary shower begins by feeling the water on the back of your hand, not on your whole body. A heat wave comes from the stickiness under the arm. A tiny detail opens the door to the larger picture.

Spheres of Attention

We do not store our memories one at a time, chronologically. Instead, everything that is similar or related is lumped together. That's why we sometimes slip and say *fire truck* when we mean *ambulance;*

the concepts of vehicles with sirens are stored close together in the brain. The memory of the cup of coffee is stored in our brains next to the experience of our kitchen, making breakfast, related concepts like cups of tea, and so on. The simple act of re-creating the action of making coffee can call forth a wealth of related details. This is so universally true that Stanislavski used it as the basis for one of his concentration techniques.

He suggested that you think of yourself being surrounded by three concentric spheres, the first one the size of your lap, the second one the size of you and a partner on stage, the final sphere stretching to the edges of the room, or if "outdoors," to the horizon.

Whenever you initiate work, he said, begin in the first sphere, concentrating on a detail that is very close to you (in your lap or just in front of you). When it is created strongly enough it will of its own accord lead you into the second sphere, and that, when sufficiently established, will lead on to the final sphere. A small detail will create the larger world.

> According to the plot of the play, you have to kill your rival. . . .
> Concentrate on the physical action; i.e., this is when you are already working on a scene with an actual prop, examining the knife; look at it closely, test its edge with your finger, find out whether its handle is firm or not. Transfer it mentally into the heart or chest of your rival; if you play the villain, try to estimate the force of the blow which will be needed to thrust the knife into your rival's back. Try to think whether you will be able to deal the blow. All your thoughts are concentrated on one subject only: the knife, the weapon.
>
> When you have gathered all your power of thought on the knife, you can begin to widen the circle of your concentrated thought. Do not attempt to change anything in your state of mind, but transfer the thought from the knife to its object; in this case, to your rival. Here your thought will stumble by itself upon the memory of your first suspicion, when he who is now your enemy was your friend.
>
> Do not change the circle. Widen it. Let your thoughts sink deep into your memories. Allow your memory, your thought, to paint you the picture of your former friendship with your rival. You have concentrated hard on your memories, you forgot all about your knife, it is still in your hand, suddenly you cut your hand with it and all those beautiful thoughts fortified by the bright picture of your past are shattered. Your attention is once

more reverted to the knife. And a whole gamut of new feelings which are now aroused by the memories of your rival's betrayal, deceit, and lies start tormenting you. (Stanislavski, quoted in Strasberg 1987, 55–56)

This simple technique, finding a small sensation that can be widened to create an imaginary environment, is the key to approaching a script so that it will come to life rather than be a set of speeches. Once you have learned to do it, it is deceptively easy. It induces thought at very deep levels, but may feel more relaxing than taxing!

If my students have a common difficulty, it is not with learning this exercise, but with *accepting* it. Many comment that it feels too easy. They note that the results are beyond their conscious intentions. They often feel as if they are cheating. It takes some time for them to accept that they have abilities within them of which they were not aware.

Rest assured that you are not cheating. This is, in fact, hard work. The work, however, is in inducing the proper frame of mind. The results come from staying on track mentally, not from concentrating on the image of the intended result.

Journal Entry: Creating an Environment

In Chapter 4, you were instructed to make journal entries about your ability to perceive sensation in the creative state. This chapter is about almost the same thing, but with a small difference: you are now also *creating* sensation.

Make notes to yourself about your ability to do this. What kinds of problems does this task present? What questions do you have about the process? What do you notice about your creative state when you use it in this active way? Are you having any emotional reactions to this exercise? What are they? (More on this subject appears in Chapter 6.)

Also write a note or two to yourself about the shift from reacting to sensation to causing it. Were you able to feel and respond to sensations that you were also causing? Did you find that you were able, as suggested by Stanislavski's circles-of-attention exercise, to extrapolate a sense of place and time from just a few details? How do these sensations feel to you? They are, of course, coming from your imagination. Can you find a way to describe the feeling of a recalled sensation? How is it similar to, and how does it differ from, physical sensation in the everyday world?

Related Optional Exercises

1. Do the exercise described in Stanislavski's circle-of-attention story. Create an environment and a relationship by expanding your attention from a single prop.
2. Concentrate on a single point close to you, the corner of a table for example. Keep your attention on this point while you relax your body. Focus on this one spot until you are fascinated with it and are firmly in the creative state. Slowly allow your attention to widen to include perhaps the tabletop, but keep the same sharp focus on detail. Now you are looking at a larger area with the same intensity of concentration as you were the table corner. Slowly allow your circle to widen until your concentration breaks. Think of it as a balloon. See how far you can expand this intense concentration until it can no longer stretch. Expand slowly to keep the balloon from bursting. See if you can take in the whole table, the whole room, perhaps the whole building! When your balloon pops, begin again and see if you can get further this time.
3. Do the same ordinary activity for three different reasons. Pound on a tabletop, for example. Imagine the given circumstance is that you are trying to quiet an angry crowd for a senate hearing on a controversial subject. Start over. This time pound on the table to test its steadiness. See if it would hold you while you climbed up on it to change a light bulb. Start over. Pound on the table to awaken a friend who has fallen asleep on it. Imagine you are angry with him, perhaps for getting drunk and passing out at your party. Change the circumstance: imagine that you feel sorry for him, because you know he is exhausted, but that he must go take a final exam or he will flunk a course. Don't overthink what you are doing, but notice how changing circumstances alter the manner in which you carry out the task.
4. Create a physical sensation in yourself to which you can respond. For instance, create a toothache by imagining some-

one scraping your gums with a razor blade. Or close your eyes and create a tickling on your skin by imagining a spider crawling up your arm. Notice the reality of your reaction to these imaginary circumstances.

6   Emotion and Feeling

Few topics in acting are as controversial as the question of emotion. The school that Stanislavski founded was noted for its emotional honesty in performance and the emphasis laid upon it in training. The American variations on his system spent great deals of time on creating and expressing emotion. Lee Strasberg, in particular, was said to be obsessed with the subject.

Looking at the question historically, this focus is hardly surprising. Before Stanislavski, the predominant acting style trained actors to induce emotion through assuming specific poses that, through a kind of proto-Pavlovian training, the actor had learned to associate with specific personal emotions. Some actors were brilliant at doing this. Upon seeing a performance by the one genuinely "Del Sarte"–trained actor I've ever met, I found much less to ridicule than I had been led to expect. The problem, however, was that most actors of Stanislavski's time had never been formally trained. They learned through observation and then imitated the performances of the stars of their time. With little appreciation for process, they outwardly adopted the well-known postures as shortcut indications of the emotions rather than inducing anything in themselves. Emotion was widely rendered symbolically, leading to the kind of hoary clichés we associate with melodrama: lustful twirling of mustaches and fainting damsels with the backs of their hands pressed delicately to their fore-heads. When layered over a Victorian literature that was emotionally repressed, sexist, and sentimental, the lack of truth was galling.

In that context, Stanislavski and his fellow reformers had an enormous task. The need to overthrow a complacent convention-ality about *indicating* emotions on the stage meant they had to be insistent about creating emotional truth in the theatre until achiev-ing a paradigm change. That took a long time. Even once Stanislavski had won his actors over to a theoretical view that favored creating genuine emotion over symbolic representations of it, the emotional constrictions of the era left many of them with few life skills to express themselves truthfully. In the classroom, Stanislavski's assistants spent much time and effort on creating emotionally responsive instruments in actors whose lives before the classroom had done little to prepare them to be either honest or revealing about their emotions.

Lagging some twenty years behind their European counter-parts in reform, American trainers found a situation in the twenties and thirties in the United States that paralleled the state of the the-atre Stanislavski had faced in Russia at the beginning of his work. Stage performers were used to indicating their emotional states with highly conventionalized postures and hand positions. Popular theatre literature was melodramatically sentimental about mom and apple pie, and puritanically repressed about almost all the rest of human emotionality in fear perhaps that it might somehow lead to an honest discussion of sexuality.

In order to facilitate the new kind of actor serving the new modern drama, American schools of acting found themselves repeat-ing the Russian pattern of insistent drilling of emotional production to overthrow the conventional external approach and to psycholog-ically enable actors to escape their personal emotional constric-tions. This training bordered on psychotherapy in the more inten-sive studios.

Why is emotional acting controversial? For two reasons: First, the performance related issue is that some actors became so enam-ored of their emotional technique that their acting became more about personal display than the truth of the character or the inten-tions of the playwright. They valued their emotionality to the point that it became a fixation supplanting all other parts of preparing their role. Demanding conditions conducive to melodramatic emoting, their public image was that they were *prima donnas*. Actors prone to this failing, even if they were a small subgroup, have historically been "Method" actors. For this reason, many actors with good training and better judgment are unfortunately reluctant to be publicly identified with the Stanislavski system, even while privately applying its principles. Second is the training-related issue: some coaches doggedly pursued emotional release beyond all theatrical application, to the point that they were manipulative and domineering. Abuses of pseudopsychological technique in theatre training, while never widespread, were once common enough that actors legitimately began to reject these excesses as inappropriate. Unfortunately, all actor training was tarred with the same brush in the backlash against this personally invasive training.

Much has changed in the century since Stanislavski began his work. The modernists have clearly carried the day. The old acting school of stock gestures and poses is so long past that performance historians are rushing to find the last living actors who were trained in that bygone era to interview them and capture their historical approach before it is lost forever. The popular literature of our time, which remains (at least in action-oriented cinema and afternoon television) pretty melodramatic, can not be said to be emotionally repressed. On the contrary, it is shamelessly indulgent about emotional display.

It seems wildly unfair to ridicule turn-of-the-century Russian training, or even midcentury American training, as obsessive when it faced such different societal and theatrical circumstances. It is valid, however, that we reexamine the place of emotional process training in the current theatre given our changed attitudes and standards. What was necessary then might be overkill now. What grew excessive, in the hands of some well-meaning but uninformed trainers, ought to be reviewed. What was perpetrated in the name of the most advanced science and psychiatry of that time might appear primitive, even detrimental, with the latest information in hand.

Reconsidering Emotion Cognitively

In some sense, the process of feeling our emotions is not very difficult, but the cognitive process underlying it is amazingly complex. It was not well understood even at the time that this book's first edition was published (early 1990s.) Only at the millennium's turn has it begun to be biologically explainable. This is largely because both science and philosophy distrusted emotion and its power to sway the logical mind. Both fields tended to underestimate it and therefore avoid it as a research subject. (Some of the intellectual prejudice against emotion underlies the controversies in acting, but it would be unfair to say that this prejudice is solely responsible for the wavering reputation of emotional process training in the theatre.) It is primarily in the last decade that some of medicine's and science's big names, most notably neurobiologist Antonio Damasio, have undertaken new research and begun to explain the importance of feeling in human cognition.

What are emotions? Though most of us can label our emotions, we have trouble saying exactly what they are. Just for the record, there is uncommon agreement that there are six primary emotional labels: happiness, sadness, surprise, disgust, fear, and anger. These are universal and noticeable even in infants. Beyond that there are a host of more socially oriented emotions like embarrassment, jealousy, love, and guilt, which are culturally specific. For this reason there is not a definitive list of these. Some psychologists go on to make a distinction between these secondary emotions and some further "states of being," like calmness or anxiety.

Biologically speaking, Damasio tells us, emotions are chemical and neural responses in the brain, which cluster together to form a pattern used by our deepest self to assist in preserving our life as an organism. It may seem unhelpful at first to resort to such a cold, scientific definition of emotion, but by doing so we can see a crucial point. Emotions are organic, that is, part of the normal operation of the organism. This is a very important distinction that Stanislavski instinctively understood, and his clarity on this point informed his entire approach to acting. Emotions are not artificial creations subject to easy manipulation. They are natural responses that obey organic laws. To train our emotional technique, we will have to understand those organic laws and use them, since it is not possible to work outside or around them.

Recent researchers would add two more points to this understanding that will have implications for our acting. These chemical and neural processes are the emotion, and they are separate from our *feeling* that emotion. Feelings are a step above emotion, a separate cognitive process whereby our body is impacted by the emotion. We often use the words *feeling* and *emotion* interchangeably, but biologically feelings are the way emotions separately register in our body. The most important point that can be made about feelings and emotions from an acting point of view is that both of these can happen below the level of consciousness. We may, and in fact often do, have chemical and neural responses to stimuli (emotions) of which we are unaware. We may even have bodily reactions to our emotions (feelings) and still remain consciously unaware of them. This is counterintuitive, but with reflection you will be able to recall occasions on which you witnessed someone being impatient for no apparent reason, and his reaction to this may have induced a petulance or annoyance of which he was unaware. I'll bet you've had occasions on which you had to ask someone *What's the matter? Why are you so moody?* only to find that he not only didn't know what the matter was, but didn't realize he was acting strangely.

For the purposes of our discussion, we have to note that the biological process happens in three layers: The first is emotion; the second is feeling. The final layer is awareness of our feelings; that is, consciously feeling our feelings.

This recently emerged model of emotion repeats significant patterns from models of cognition like the pyramid of thought in Chapter 3. Emotional processing is parallel to (and part of) work with the senses. It starts below the threshold of consciousness, is broader than what our conscious awareness of it includes, and has to be induced indirectly. Like sensory reactions, emotion is a response to a stimulus. That stimulus can be either external or internal, real or imaginary. It makes no difference to the emotional process. The emotional reaction is the same whether the stimulus is an object, a current happening, a memory, or a fantasy. The *feeling* that is invoked by the emotion is always real, whether or not the stimulus that induced the emotion was.

Knowing this, we can begin to see more clearly what is meant by Stanislavski's phrase "living truthfully in imaginary circumstances." Living truthfully means responding fully and organically to the stimuli of the play. These stimuli are "imaginary circumstances" in that they are fictional creations, but they are very real in the way in which the brain creates chemical and neural patterns in response to them.

This is in sharp contrast to a widely held misunderstanding of the technique that interprets "living truthfully" to mean responding as we habitually do to stimuli presented from the world, therefore playing ourselves at all times.

Stanislavski, himself, had to learn this lesson the hard way. One of the most contentious turning points in the history of his acting studio turned on a question of emotion. One day in the very early years, Stanislavski had come to the acting studio to observe student work on emotional exercises. He was particularly struck by the intensity and beauty of an exercise by the then-young student Michael Chekhov in re-creating his father's funeral. Chekhov not only captured the given circumstances of the wake, but organically felt his own grief and loss in an intensely moving performance. Stanislavski praised this exercise as exemplary, but within a few days he had changed his mind and was contemplating expelling Chekhov from the school. In the intervening days, it had been brought to his attention that Chekhov's father was still living. His exercise had not been an emotional re-creation of a past event, but an imaginative projection of a future one. Stanislavski felt betrayed and thought his extensive public praise of Chekhov's work made him the subject of ridicule.

Stanislavski's star student and protégé, Evgeni Vakhtangov, intervened on his fellow student's behalf. Wasn't the kind of work Chekhov had done, he asked, artistically valid? They had all been moved by the performance. Further, in performance weren't actors often called to feel emotions that they had not experienced in their real lives?

Stanislavski relented. In time he conceded this incident taught him it was not the literal truth that he was seeking, but the organic truth of the emotional response. It was not important that actors re-create actual incidents from their lives, but that they genuinely respond to stimuli, whether those stimuli be direct, called from memory or created by the imagination.

Stanislavski encoded this new understanding into his system. In Chapter 2 we saw that the fourth point of his ten-point outline dealt with the sense of truth. Stanislavski told the story of Chekhov's exercise to clarify that he meant the *organic* truth of the instrument (feeling, not faking it) but not necessarily the literal truth about our lives outside the theatre. This point was often very difficult for his disciples to understand, but with a new cognitive understanding of emotion we can see far more clearly that there is an organic truth to emotion and to our subsequent feelings.

The implication of a cognitive understanding of emotion is this: creating feeling is not something you do as an actor but a by-product of what you do. It will arise naturally, and on cue, if you are in the creative state and fully pursuing your objectives in the scene. If you are working with your senses fully engaged, and are in touch with the given circumstances of the play, the neural and chemical messages that form emotional patterns in the brain happen without your conscious willing of them.

There are, however, two questions dealing with emotion that have to be addressed.

The first is, what do you do when feelings do arise? *Nothing*. Real emotion is preconscious. You don't will feeling but make the conditions for it. If you make the right circumstances to stimulate emotion, feeling will follow.

Actually, there is one thing you should do—remember to take a breath. Continue whatever you were doing, especially attending to what you were concentrating on when you felt the stirrings of feelings.

Most of us, when going about our everyday business, find strong feelings inappropriate or intrusive. We are quite good at feeling these first warning signals and immediately shutting down our emotional impulses. We hold our breath, think of something else, and wait for the emotion to pass. To allow it to flourish, you want to avoid these interfering steps.

While rehearsing, and later when performing, you needn't do anything about emotion and feeling except allow it. It lives on breath. As long as you continue your actions and keep the oxygen flowing, it will rise and blossom.

The second question is, when emotion does arise will you be able to handle it? The answer to this is an unequivocal yes. The fact is, though many of us don't know this from direct experience, we usually stop emotions before they manifest out of fear they will overwhelm us. Few people ever just indulge emotion to know how the resulting feeling naturally rises and falls again.

Many beginning actors worry that if they begin to feel strong emotions, especially the unpleasant four flavors of the primary emotions (anger, fear, disgust, and sadness), they will never be able to stop them. They fear they will "lose control," and perhaps feel this way for the rest of their lives. Many people have very strong qualms about this. One of my best students once confided in me, after I asked what it was about the process she feared, that she was afraid if she really let herself feel her reaction to something that had happened to her she would become so angry it would kill her. Literally.

That is a big fear! If there were any danger that your emotions could kill you, it would be a good reason for having little traffic with them. It is more likely that the opposite is true, however. Refusal to allow feelings and repressing them is bad for you. Experiencing your feelings is not. Emotional states, being chemical and neural events, are not permanent. No one in all of history has become locked into an emotional state as the result of a single stimulus and never come out of it again. Emotions rise in organic waves and fall again. They usually do so rather quickly, but sometimes these waves last for ten to fifteen minutes the very first time strong reactions to powerful stimuli are allowed to flourish.

Until you allow a few of them to occur in the safety of rehearsal, in the presence of partners you trust, you won't know the truth of this assertion. Discovering your emotional process is something you will find through action, just as you learned to perceive better and express yourself better.

Creating emotion is not under your direct control, but interestingly, emotional states are delicate enough that interfering with them *is* under your control. Just focusing on another stimulus can end one. The acting problem is *allowing* feeling when it does come. You will learn this better through direct experience using the following exercise.

emotional memory exercise

learning about feelings

This exercise takes about twenty minutes. Set an alarm or ask someone else to keep track of the time.

1. Begin as you did with the sensory exploration exercise, using a simple object that stimulates several of the senses, but which also has some personal meaning to you. It might be a gift from a loved one, a personal diary or photograph, or a childhood toy, for example.
2. Just as you did in the previous exercise, sit in a comfortable chair with your hands resting in your lap, the object in your

hands. Don't use a desk or a table. Begin to shift the object around slightly and note the various feelings you are experiencing, paying particular attention to emotional feelings as well as physical ones.

3.　Identify in your mind the specific time and place you first knew this object was important to you. This might be your first encounter with the object, but often it is later that we come to understand the meaning of something. A gift from a grandmother, for example, is apt to become poignantly meaningful as a reminder and a link after her death. Fix this time and place in your mind. Do not shift around in your mind to other times and places or you will find yourself as confused as if you were rapidly changing objects.

4.　Without worrying about creating emotion or other outcomes, concentrate on the remembered sensations and feelings of that time and place. The object in your hands is a reminder about this time and place, but it is the sensations of the time and place itself that you are exploring. These sensations are the stimuli to which you will be reacting.

5.　With the same deliberate slowness that you used in the sensory exploration exercise, carefully recall, one at a time, the physical sensations associated with the time and place and with your feelings. (In other words, think about the knot in your stomach, not the affect of the moment.) Keep breathing regularly through the exercise.

6.　Notice the way that by deliberately concentrating on these sensations you will be drawn into the creative state. Note also that you will have a *current* reaction to a *past* event. You may not feel the same now as you did then. You are not re-creating the past, but seeing how you react now to the memorial stimuli of then. Make no effort to control your reactions; simply allow them.

7.　Slowly build sensation on sensation, exploring each individually. Keep working until you have successfully re-created the entire time and place or until the alarm sounds.

Do the exercise now, before reading on. After you have finished, evaluate your experience.

This is an exercise that cannot be forced, and the goal is not to have a spectacular emotional display. It is simply to learn that all feelings (both of physical sensation and of emotional response) are responses to stimuli. If you went slowly and made the shift to the creative state, you probably felt an emotional component to the work as well.

Student Portrait

Brent

A big, amiable guy, Brent is a former high school wrestler whose object is, as all can obviously see, the trophy he won as state champion in the sport a half dozen years ago. It seems out of place among the plethora of tiny stuffed animals, class rings, and prom photos that the rest of the students have with them. Brent is fairly open about his motive. If he is going to do work on emotion, then he is going to call up a "man's" emotion. He intends to re-create the thrill of victory, not some long-forgotten high school crush-gone-bad upon which several of his classmates seem intent. That is fine with the instructor. This exercise is not a crying contest and he is happy to have a student who is more interested in the process than making a point.

Brent is a meticulous student, and he is firmly in control of his work. He sits in the chair, examining the enormous trophy millimeter by millimeter. In short order he is drawn in and observably shifts to the creative state. The instructor urges Brent to fix upon the time and place he first knew the trophy was important to him. He blurts out, "As soon as I got it!" The instructor was not really asking him for a verbal answer, but a mental commitment. After clarifying that point he urges Brent to recall the sensations associated with the time and place. "What did you see? What could you hear? How did you physically feel?"

"Can you re-create those sensations?" the instructor asks. The class knows the answer without Brent saying a word. His face lights up. He is looking around a gymnasium that only he can see to an obvious cheering crowd. We can guess without help what he hears and sees. Uncoached, Brent stands up out of his chair and "steps up" on what must be a medal stand to receive his award. A few observant students note that the match must have taken its toll, as Brent's body is less powerful than we assumed it might be. He is apparently reliving some aches and pains.

There is no doubt that Brent is swept away with feelings, not just of the physical kind. His emotions are suddenly boiling. "Keep breathing," the instructor urges him. He takes a deep breath and suddenly what everyone thinks are tears of joy start rolling down his cheeks. In seconds, however, it is clear that Brent's feelings have taken an unexpected turn. He sits back down in his chair and quietly sobs. Gently the instructor asks him if he can say what is going on, and he answers, "I just miss it so much."

Brent keeps breathing and for more than a while he just sits crying. Eventually, however, his emotions subside and he is again calmly clearheaded. The irony has not escaped him that he was determined to be the class member who remembered a happy time, but turned out to be the only class member who cried. His evaluation is interesting, however. He knows the crying was not the point, especially since it was not what he had intended to do. It was, however, instructive.

Brent and his classmates have a discussion around something the instructor had said before the exercise. "I get it now, what you meant about having a present reaction to a past event," he tells his instructor. He identifies that he had meant to re-create the incredible elation he had felt at the moment of what he considered the biggest accomplishment of his life. But that moment is gone, and what he feels *now* is the loss of that adulation and control. What he understands more clearly is the process by which he arrived at this emotional state. Through creating the stimuli of the remembered environment he put himself in the creative state, and from there it was a matter of allowing his feelings to flow naturally wherever they wanted to go. Next time, however, Brent thinks he might have more artistic control because he will have a better sense of where this set of stimuli will lead. "Learning to act is learning the laws of your own responsiveness," his instructor says, quoting his own favorite teacher.

Denisha notes that Brent had basically carried out a sensory observation exercise but that the object had drawn emotion from him instead of just concentration. Brent agrees that the exercise was very similar, but quickly adds that except for focusing his concentration at the beginning of the exercise, he didn't really use the trophy at all. The instructor again clarifies. The power, he says, is not in the objects in this exercise nor in the sensory exploration exercise. It is always in the actor. The objects are just reminders of times and places, a way to begin working. Once the actor really understands the process, he can initiate it without using any objects at all.

Warning Notes

Knowing that emotional work is just another flavor of sensory work takes much of its mystery away—a good thing from an actor's perspective. There are a few warnings worth adding, however.

Because of the prevalence of focus on emotion in psychotherapy, some actors assume that the acting classroom will serve as therapy for them. It doesn't, not least because the instructor is not certified as a therapist. More important, the aim of emotional work, as can't be repeated too often, is not display for its own sake. In the theatre it will become a tool to fully create character and serve plays. The preceding exercise is not concerned with any therapeutic outcome, and doesn't have one even if you find yourself expressing strong emotion. Some actors find themselves occasionally dealing with emotional stimuli that they feel they "can't handle." While emotion is not dangerous, it is worth noting that we develop psychological defenses in relation to some emotionally loaded situations for a reason. You might ultimately want to seek professional guidance in confronting this defense, but the classroom is not the place for it. Good instructors will not "break down" your defenses; they'll refer you to someone who might assist you with your psychological issues separately. In the meantime, they'll steer you back to learning the laws of your own responsiveness, including finding stimuli that you can artistically control and utilize.

Some schools of thought about acting encourage actors to find precise parallels to their characters' emotions in plays and essentially squeeze an emotional memory exercise into the confines of the play. This process is sometimes called *substitution* or *emotional recall*. As a training technique there is some validity to the approach, but it is extremely dubious as a performance technique. The popularity of this practice actually grew in relation to film work, where it can take hours to set up a shot and then great pressure is placed on an actor to deliver emotional outpourings in short time frames with little preparation. Because the filming of a two-hour story can be spread over months, the plot incidents leading to the emotion are not in the actor's immediate experience. In real time they may have been filmed weeks before, or are yet to be filmed at a later date. Fifties film actors, especially, used emotional recall exercises on the set to get themselves ready. It was never really a theatrical technique.

Journal Entry: Emotion and Feeling

In the last chapters you learned to work with sensation and to create stimuli. Emotional work is an extension of this same idea, the only difference being the nature of the stimuli with which you are working. Try to explain the parallel nature of these processes in your journal using examples from your own exercise work or broader experience.

Make notes in your journal about the way in which you become aware of the physical sensations attached with emotional reactions in your body. How and where does emotion arise in you, and can you sense a pattern to the way it occurs?

Though we label emotions when we see them in others, we often perceive them in very mixed states in ourselves. (Lovesickness is so labeled because most of us don't experience romance as pure joy, for example, but as dangerous risk taking and worrisome gambling occurring simultaneously with our current happiness.) When emotion results in feeling in you, does it feel physically different for each emotion, or does it feel similar across emotions? Make notes in your journal for future reference about the process of allowing emotion to blossom into feeling and any problems you may be encountering.

7 Adding Speech

Ordinarily when we speak in public, we are working almost entirely from our analytic mode of thought. This task is perfectly suited to logical processing. Public speaking is largely the process of finding appropriate verbal symbols (words) to convey our mental abstractions (ideas). Language and abstraction are both logical specialties. When giving an oral report to a class, speaking to a group, or reciting a memorized piece, we are in a state almost completely opposite of that experienced in sensory exploration. Sensory exploration is the process of reliving an experience by re-creating its sensory impact; typical public speaking is almost devoid of sensory awareness. It is only minimally important to pay attention to our senses in such a situation. Even when we are discussing something that has previously happened to us, it is not relevant to relive the experience. We can and do discuss it in very detached ways. The communication from speaker to audience is almost completely made up of symbolic interactions.

Actors in a play are of course speaking in public, but they do so in a way quite different from the public speaker. They are not dispassionately removed from what they are saying. They do not recite or lecture. They do not remove themselves from their sensory environment. Actors bring life to the words they speak. The actors' words sound like they are being invented on the spot, being spoken for the first time. The interaction between actor and audience is considerably more varied and complex than that between public speaker and audience. The words are not the whole of the actors' message as they are the speaker's, but only a part of the total communication.

Therefore actors do not use the strategies of public speaking. They use the rich sensory awareness of the creative state studied in Chapters 4 and 5. Rather than turning off the creative state and switching over to public speaking, actors have to find a way to speak their lines without giving up the foundation provided by the bottom layer of the pyramid of thought—the sensory layer.

From our studies of the hemispheric specialties of the brain, we know this to be a complicated process. Speaking is largely a dominant hemisphere function. This hemisphere usually overrides and inhibits the minor one. The previous chapters have taught us to learn to function in the creative state by evading logical interference: by boring or confusing the dominant hemisphere and especially by silencing it. As we begin to add speech to our work, we must face the problem in a new way.

Of all the actor's tasks, speaking has the most hidden traps. So much about the situation calls forth old habits, launching us into logical thought before we are consciously aware of it. Because the dominant hemisphere is especially equipped to handle speech, because that is how we are used to verbalizing, because that is the way we have always been trained, it is inclined to take over.

> *People can be forgiven for overrating language. Words make noise, or sit on the page, for all to hear and see. Thoughts are trapped inside the head of the thinker. To know what someone else is thinking or to talk to each other about the nature of thinking, we have to use— what else, words! It is no wonder that many commentators have trouble even conceiving of thought without words—or is it that they just don't have the language to talk about it?*
> —Steven Pinker

Of course, good actors do successfully conquer this challenge. We can too, and, like learning to work in the creative state, it is exciting doing so. We learn more about the capabilities of our mind. Good actors learn to think in a unique way that while primarily based in the sensory layer, allows a bit of the verbal layer of thought to be added to the sensory grounding. This method is a kind of dual mental processing, in which both modes of thought interact, called *double tracking*.

Double Tracking

Double tracking allows the actor to balance the logical and creative modes of thought by focusing on the *context* of the speech rather than concentrating exclusively on its content. The context of the speech includes such matters as the environment in which it is being spoken, the person(s) to whom it is addressed, underlying meanings that may only be hinted at by the literal definitions of the words, and the mood and intent of the speaker.

Contextual matters are considerably more sensory than matters of content, which tend to be abstract ideas. Contextual matters therefore tend to be more in line with your creative thought processes. By approaching language obliquely at first, you can train yourself not to be trapped by your old speaking habits. This gives you a way to see the life that underlies language freshly, without the clouding influence of symbols. The first step toward this may be experienced in a variation on the sensory exploration exercise.

> **verbal/sensory exploration exercise I**
>
> **describing sensory exploration**

This exercise will take about twenty minutes. Set an alarm or ask someone else to monitor the time so that you will not have to. This exercise may be performed before a class or group, but do not feel obligated to demonstrate for them or talk directly to them.

1. Choose a common everyday object like the one you used in the sensory exploration exercise.
2. Sit in a comfortable chair with your hands in your lap, the object in your hands.
3. Precisely as before, begin a sensory exploration by identifying the strongest sensation from the object and working to maximize it.
4. As you work, begin describing the exact concrete sensations you are experiencing. For example, you might say about a soft drink can you are holding: *I feel the pressure on my fingertips. I notice a coolness on my palm. I feel the liquid on the front of my tongue, then it moves around the edges of my tongue to my*

throat. *I feel a slight burning as it goes down my throat.*
Whenever possible, tie your descriptions to the part of the
body that is experiencing the sensation.

5. *Avoid* running descriptions of your actions: *I am drinking it*
    now. Now I taste it, etc. The sequential, time-based nature of
    such descriptions favors the dominant hemisphere function
    that we are trying to avoid. Do what you can to avoid labeling
    the sensations. *It is cold* is less useful than *I feel the* (unla-
    belled) *sensation* (of coldness) *on my palm.*

6. Work continuously, and talk while working. Watch out for
    the tendency to explore a bit, then stop to talk, and then
    explore again. This is not an exercise in alternating logical
    and creative modes. It is an exercise in learning to do both *at*
    the same time.

7. Continue the process of sensory exploration with commen-
    tary until the alarm sounds or time is up.

Do the exercise now, before reading further.

Student Portraits

Kim

Kim is so excited about the exercise that, ironically, she is having
trouble doing it. She wants to tell us about her subjective responses
rather than the object. "I brought in liver," she says midexercise,
"because I hate it so much I knew I'd have a big response." At the
moment, however, she is not having the promised big response
nor, in fact, any response. She is telling us about her expectations
of the exercise, but she is not doing it.

Her instructor says that later he will be interested in Kim's evaluation of her work, but now he wants her to actually do the work,
not talk about it. She agrees to try to stay focused, but moments later
she is back to observing, "This is interesting."

This is a common pitfall, and after a moment of reflection, the
instructor realizes that Kim has fallen into it for the most common
of reasons—because she has not taken time to shift into the creative
state before beginning to speak. She is still in her logical mode.

Instructed to slow down and have an experience before trying
to verbally describe it, she instantly improves. Soon she is having the

promised big reaction. Kim is very responsive to the stimuli of the raw liver.

The exercise now looks entirely different. Kim is very concentrated on her object. Her instructor has asked her to take her time, but after a couple of minutes he realizes that Kim is so engrossed in exploring the object, she has forgotten to speak. As quietly as he can, so as not to disturb her, he whispers to her to try to verbalize her exploration. Kim looks slightly annoyed and then very slowly she moves toward speech. It is almost comic. Kim seems on the verge of speaking three or four times, but no sound comes out. Finally, on her fifth attempt at speech she gets out a choppy and ungrammatical phrase. Her first couple of sentences are barely comprehensible. She makes up onomatopoetic words: "I feel the oozy gooshiness." It is all quite unlike the carefully constructed Kim we see every day. Kim's voice is somewhat lower than the group has usually heard it, and it seems to be coming from somewhere far away. Slowly her descriptions gather momentum. Words come faster. Her voice is powerful and dynamic.

Kim is more intrigued than anyone when the exercise is finished. She does not say any of the things she seemed to think were so important when she was beginning. Now she is simple and direct. "This is not the way I usually thought when I acted in the past. I felt like I was in a different place. I resented you making me talk. Once I started to speak I felt like I couldn't think of the words. It seemed so hard to start speaking, but once I did I realized that this is how I feel when I am trying to explain something for the first time, or when I am trying to find the words to describe an emotion. I realized that when I am thinking through things for the first time, I do this naturally. I never paid any attention to it until now. I valued my sensations, and the funny thing is, I didn't care if they were big or spectacular or interesting to the class, or anything. I valued them all. I just wanted to keep going."

Kim and her classmates have learned something about a way to approach theatrical dialogue from a direction that does not discard or ignore the creative state. "You kind of sneak up on the words," says one.

Amy

Amy's experience is similar to Kim's. She has trouble at first concentrating on her object. She wants to rush into speech. Once she slows down and focuses on her object, she, too, has trouble getting words to form.

(It is a pattern that is to be very common in this class. They get to the point where they are counting the number of attempts it takes to get to speech. The class record belongs to Sam, who came to the verge of speech seventeen times before he got the words out. Everyone is in a different place in his or her brain, literally, and it takes a bit of time to find how to connect to the word place.)

When she gets to speech, Amy suddenly veers away from descriptions of concrete sensations and begins to narrate the steps of the exercise as she goes through them. This is dangerous, because this step-by-step narration builds the conditions for a sudden mental shift into logical thought and these conditions are the opposite of those needed to induce the creative state. Amy finds herself suddenly out of the creative state. She grinds to a complete halt and suddenly blushes bright red, self-conscious and embarrassed.

She needs to start over, and stick to sensation. Once she does, she is fine. Her exercise is very sound. She, too, experiences the lower, freer voice and the new way of thinking.

Amy is able to put into words her discovery that the terrible stage fright she sometimes experiences is a product of being in the logical rather than the creative state. For the first time, she sees the importance of building conditions that keep her in the sensory layer of thought. The benefits go far beyond just greater attention to detail, but also include greater self-confidence and security.

The Playwright's Words

Because the layer of thought employed by public speakers—the logical layer—is nearly opposite to that employed by actors creating given circumstances—the sensory layer—there is a tendency for actors to believe they need to choose one or the other. Knowing plays primarily as a set of speeches to memorize and repeat, most beginning actors find themselves giving up everything they have studied previously as soon as they begin to speak, because they don't know how to do both at once.

Trained actors, however, find the connection between the layers. They find a way to use both simultaneously. This is the premise behind the thought pyramid. In our everyday lives, we think in a wholistic way that employs each successive layer of thought in concert with the previous layers. Our brains expend a specific amount of energy on each layer. The sensory layer is the most fundamental, and it is given the greatest amount of commitment and energy. The social layer, which we use when we are interacting with other people, is given the second largest amount of energy. The verbal layer (the first layer of which we are conscious) is employed to a smaller degree. The point on the pyramid, the smallest and least-used layer, is the logical layer of thought we use to plan and organize our lives.

That was the premise behind the last activity, as well. It was an exercise in concentrating on the context of one's speech as well as the content, creating a sensory connection. Great actors maintain this feeling of sensory connectedness throughout their performances. *Sensory awareness is not a beginning exercise to be set aside once learned or used occasionally when the play demands it. It is a mode of work that underlies all performance.*

Just because this state is not familiar to us as we practice speech, it does not follow that it is unusual in our everyday life. We are in this mode of thought more often than we are in the public speaking mode, but because it is largely unconscious, we are usually unaware that we have entered it. Of course, speaking the words supplied by the playwright is not precisely parallel to narrating our own sensory exercises, but it is much closer than most laypeople imagine. The following exercise is designed to help make you a bit more aware of this state as a regular phenomenon.

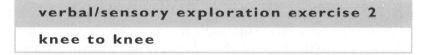

verbal/sensory exploration exercise 2

knee to knee

This exercise will take about fifteen minutes. It requires the presence of another person, but he or she will not be doing anything but listening to you. You will need a one- or two-minute speech from a play.

1. In a pair of chairs, sit facing the person who will assist you in this exercise, with your knees almost touching his or hers. (Your chairs should be about an arm's length apart.)

2. Read the speech to your assistant. This should not be prepared or memorized, just read.
3. When you have finished say, "This is what that speech was
   about." Then, in your own words, explain the content of the
   speech to your assistant.
4. Finally, read the speech again, but this time before you speak
   the first line, quickly memorize it. Just look at the first phrase
   of the speech and memorize it on the spot. Hold this information in your head for a second, look up from the script, look
   directly into your assistant's eyes and *say* (not read) the line
   to him or her. Now look at your script again and quickly
   learn the second phrase of the speech. Look up at your assistant, make eye contact, and say the second line. Continue in
   this manner, one line at a time, until you have completed the
   speech. Don't worry if you get lost occasionally and have to
   take a second to find your place. Don't say anything to excuse
   yourself; just find your place again and continue.

Do the exercise now, before reading further.

In this exercise you are dealing with the playwright's words in three
ways. The first is verbal, just voicing what is on the page. The second
is logical, paraphrasing the material, which requires you to analyze it.
The final one uses the double-tracking technique of working sensorially and verbally simultaneously. (There is also a social element to
this exercise, because you are using a partner, but because the partner is passive and silent we won't consider the social layer until later.)

Concentrating now only on how the three iterations *felt*, which
two were most alike? Which one was most unlike the others? Nine
out of ten people respond to this exercise by saying the final two iterations felt similar, with the first—the reading—feeling quite different. You need to think of the words before saying them in the final
two vocalizations, whereas in the first the presenter is practically not
present. "Transparent" was how one of my students described himself in the first iteration. This is not the only reaction, but it is the
most common one.

Think for a minute about whether you notice a difference in the
way you convey information when you are reading it, when you are
paraphrasing it, and when you are saying it to someone. This exer-

cise is designed to help you notice the way you function in life. Most of us would say, if asked in advance, that our thought processes would be quite similar during the first two steps in this exercise. In practice, however, very few people *feel* this way when they try it. Most of us notice that paraphrasing the speech requires several steps: deciding what the speech meant, how we will put it into our own words, and what words to choose, then finally saying the words. The smoothness we experience in the reading seems familiar, because that is all we are usually aware of; but when we compare it to the actual practice of thinking of what to say from scratch, it proves to be quite different. The final step is more likely to feel similar to the second step than the first is.

> *The idea that thought is the same thing as language is an example of what can be called a conventional absurdity: a statement that goes against all common sense but that everyone believes because they dimly recall having heard it somewhere and because it is so pregnant with implications. . . . We have all had the experience of uttering or writing a sentence, then stopping and realizing that it wasn't exactly what we meant to say. To have that feeling there has to be a "what we meant to say" that is different from what we said*
> —Steven Pinker

Also notice how differently you had to treat your assistant as soon as you began to paraphrase the speech to him or her. When reading, we can keep our assistants comfortably distant. We read *at* them. As soon as we paraphrase the speech, we have to speak *to* them. It is a very different sensation.

Don't worry if this was not your exact reaction to the exercise. The presence of another person, keeping our place in the script, and other externals over which we have little control can make us experience this exercise in many different ways. For now, see if you can identify the experience of creating speech as opposed to reading or repeating. If this distinction is clear, then you understand the underlying principle of the actor's task when speaking dialogue.

Actors don't quit doing the "sensory thing" when they begin speaking. They add to it. So do we, in life. The feeling of talking *to* the assistant instead of *at* her or him is a process of sensory connection. Thinking about what to say, instead of just repeating or reading the ideas, is a natural, wholistic process. Isn't this what we usually do? Unless it is brought to our attention, however, we rarely notice that we are doing so much.

Student Portrait

Marcus

At last, Marcus is getting to act. He has shared with a few friends in the group that he is tired of the "touchy-feely" stuff. He wants to get to the real thing—plays. Today is his day. His instructor has asked everyone to bring in a one- or two-minute speech from a play. Marcus had his eye on a Shakespearean soliloquy and was a bit disappointed when the instructor urged him to bring in something more contemporary. He has found a good speech from a Pulitzer prize–winning playwright, however, and his hand is the first one in the air when his instructor asks for a volunteer to do some work.

The instructor chooses him, and he comes to the front of the space, where there is a chair facing the group. Marcus sits while the teacher asks him to read the speech to the class, but he stands up to deliver it. His reading is dramatic and exciting. Marcus is clearly making the most of his chance. He has prepared it, even though he wasn't instructed to do so. He uses his best radio announcer voice, and has built several interesting vocal effects, including a haunting whisper, into the presentation.

The instructor tells Marcus he was good. Marcus glows. Next the instructor asks Marcus to paraphrase the speech. Interestingly, Marcus sits back down. As instructed, he begins by saying, "This is what the speech says." The next sound out of his mouth is *umm*. He goes on, "Well, umm, this guy is saying. . . ."

The instructor stops him: instead of narrating the speech, which risks depersonalizing it, could he just put the ideas of the speech into his own words? Marcus agrees to give it a shot. He pulls the copy of the speech a little closer, where he can consult it easily. He looks over the first sentence and then looks up at the instructor and says, "It means that I was riding in the car with my dad." That is a simple and direct paraphrase of the line, but the instructor is still not quite satisfied. He is worried about that little disclaimer at the start—the "it means." Just like putting this in the third person, this phrase seems to push Marcus apart from the speech. His instructor wants him to take more ownership of it. He explains this to Marcus and gets him to say, "I was riding in a car with my dad." Marcus then looks at the script to get the second sentence in his mind, and paraphrases it. He is doing well, so the instructor motions for Marcus to finish the job but direct it to the group instead of to the instructor personally.

It takes a while, and nearly every sentence starts with *umm,* but Marcus does it well. He looks noticeably relieved when the instructor says he is to go on to the third part of the exercise, where he will be using the script directly again.

The instructor asks Marcus to deliver the speech to the class again, but this time to memorize the script one line at a time and look up from the page to deliver each line. He is to fix on one classmate and deliver the line especially to him or her. He may choose a different person for each line, but each one is to be specifically delivered to someone.

Marcus already half-knows the speech, so the process goes more quickly than usual. He doesn't even have to look down at the first line. Oddly enough, however, he doesn't look at anybody when he delivers it. He seems to be saying it to the crowd generally. The instructor immediately interrupts him and asks him to be sure to look right at someone for the next line.

"Do I have to?" Marcus asks.

Intrigued, the instructor asks him why he doesn't want to.

"It's messing me up," Marcus replies.

"What is it messing up?"

"The way I want to say the line," Marcus answers immediately.

The instructor reiterates that he wants Marcus to do the exercise as requested, but that they can talk a bit about the way it "messes him up" afterward. With that promise, Marcus tries again.

He is still having difficulty, so the instructor asks Jennifer to pull up a chair and sit knee to knee with Marcus so he has someone very close to him to focus on. "Say all the lines to her," the instructor tells him.

Finally Marcus is able to do the exercise, looking at each line of the speech, instantly memorizing it, and then speaking it to Jennifer. The lines sound nothing like they did the first time he read them. They tell a different story altogether.

Marcus obviously doesn't like the reading, and says so afterward. Prompted by the instructor, he says it's because here was another time he didn't get to act.

"I agree," the instructor says, surprising him. "You didn't act at all." Because they were outside the experience, the group understands the instructor's irony, but Marcus can't.

Jennifer jumps in to try to explain. "The first time you didn't really act, you read it. It was good, but it wasn't real. No offense,

Marcus, but it was kind of fake. You did some good stuff with your voice, but it was storytelling, not acting. You seemed really angry about the whole scene. When you just said it to me it was simpler, but you were there. It wasn't fake and far away. It was right to me. I didn't understand until after the last time that this is a story about a guy who feels hurt. I heard the whole thing in a new way. It was much better."

"If I hadn't seen you do the second performance, I would have really liked the first time, but when I saw the other way, I realized how planned and manipulative your 'acting' was," Barry chimes in.

It is pretty clear that everyone feels the same way. They dislike the very thing that Marcus is proudest of—his carefully structured effects. These are technically effective, but they are neither organic nor truthful. Marcus' planning shows, and makes his performance seem artificial.

For some time Marcus withstands the onslaught. Despite the fact that every one of the group sees something extraordinary in, and therefore prefers, his second performance, he is certain that his first attempt was better. Finally, the instructor asks Marcus why he is so sure of his judgment. "Because," he says, making a very intriguing distinction, "I was in control of *my* reading, but *your* exercise was just random."

Through a series of musings, though, Marcus begins to come around to a different view of his work. Marcus, himself, puts together that his planned reading was too directly symbolic to be convincing, but that it felt good to him because he felt so communicative. He sent a message and received the pleasure of knowing it got through. The difficulty is that good acting is more than just a symbolic communication. For the first performance, he was an effective messenger, but his performance did not seem to be his. It was oddly impersonal. Like a radio announcer reading the morning news, no one would ever think that this speech expressed any private thought.

Marcus is delighted to "discover" his own inner resources are also communicative, but in a much more complex and subtle way. His discussions with his classmates have revealed to him a glimpse of how powerful his connected version was, despite the fact that most of the elements were not planned but subconscious.

Marcus' experience is extreme, but in a milder form many students go through something similar. This exercise is not one that can be easily predicted or explained. It breaks down many common misunderstandings about what acting is all about. Once completed, there is often a period of disorientation before a paradigm shift occurs. Students find themselves reevaluating all their beliefs about the way their mind works and how their creative abilities are structured.

Pushing the Envelope

An Alternate Approach to Adding Speech

This exercise will take about five minutes. It is meant to be performed before a class or group. It requires a prepared monologue, one to two minutes long, memorized in advance. (For advice on selecting and memorizing a monologue, see the Resources section at the end of the book.) It also requires a simple object suitable for a sensory exploration exercise.

Before beginning, for purposes of comparison, it is very helpful to perform the monologue once trying to articulate the meaning of the words clearly to the listeners. It is not necessary to act it out; simply recite it from memory. Immediately after, with no discussion, begin the exercise.

1. Sit in a comfortable chair and begin a sensory exploration of the object selected for the exercise. Do this in the same slow, careful manner you used in previous exercises.
2. In your head, but without speaking, begin to describe your work as you did in the first verbal/sensory exploration exercise. After you have *thought* through a sentence or two, such as *I feel the coolness on my palm*, prepare to speak the third sentence out loud.
3. While continuing your sensory exploration of the object, and while *thinking* the words of your third descriptive sentence, such as *I feel the liquid roll across my tongue,* actually *speak* the first line of your monologue. Think the appropriate thought about your sensory work, but substitute the completely unrelated words of the monologue to express it out loud.
4. Note a new sensation, and again thinking the appropriate thought, use the completely unrelated second line of the monologue to express it out loud.
5. Continue until you have completed the monologue.

Of all the Stanislavski-based exercises I know, this one is the most surprising and unsettling. Like the upside-down drawing exercise, it goes against every logical assumption we have about our work, yet the results are striking and obvious.

First, it is much easier for the beginner to remember the words to the monologue in the sensory exploration phase than it is when simply reciting them. There is usually a much greater sense of calmness, and the student is very focused—benefits we could predict based on our previous experiences with the creative state.

But most shocking of all, the meaning of the speech is much clearer in the latter case, when the student is not trying to express it, than it is in the former, when it is the sole point of the recitation. In the majority of cases, it is much more specific and emotional. I have never seen it fail to be more believable, lively, and interesting. More often than not, the students reveal a clear "character" very unlike their everyday personalities, one that is more forceful and articulate.

Despite the clear differences, which are usually as obvious to the performer as to the listeners, the student-performers occasionally prefer the spoken-monologue version to the sensory exploration. It seems closer to what they think they "should" do. They are shocked that the monologue may be clearer and more interesting while they concentrate on the sensory details of the exercise than when they "express" it. They cannot, at first, accept the illogical conclusion.

Performing this exercise is often the first indication to the student of what is meant by Stanislavski's phrase "using the conscious to tap the unconscious." In this exercise the performer consciously focuses on the sensory context of the piece, and this creates conditions through which a more engaged, emotional, and detailed performance emerges than he or she consciously intended.

Journal Entry: Speaking and Feeling

Did you experience the conflict between speaking and maintaining your sensory base? If so, you might want to make a few notes about the nature of this friction. If you are aware of shifting mental states, try to pinpoint what causes the slide back toward top-down, logic-driven thinking when you are trying to maintain bottom-up, sensorially based thinking. What artistic problems are presented by this conflict? Don't feel an obligation to solve your problems in your journal; just note the conflicts that arise. If solutions naturally suggest themselves, write those down too. Open-ended and unresolved questions, however, are very legitimate journal entries. Stanislavski created a whole system out of some of his unresolved questions years after he had first noted them.

Giving a Solo Performance

I t's time to combine the various components you have been practicing in isolation into a performance. You have practiced creating
a set of given circumstances (said another way, you have practiced
creating a sense of life). You have experienced adding speech in a
way that allows you to speak while keeping your concentration on
this underlying sense of life. You have learned to avoid superficial
symbolic representations by staying in a frame of mind that calls
some of your deepest mental resources into play. You have the skills
needed for your first performance.

But there is still one step you must take. To date, these skills have
been structured by the *actor's* imagination. Now we are going to make
the first of a series of leaps that will bring us into the world imagined by the *playwright*.

This is a crucial difference. Until now, you have been instructed
to avoid the playwright's precise world, because the temptation is so
great that you will be awed by the literature and assume counter-
productive frames of mind. In the previous exercises, by using *your*
imagination you were able to experience the sensation of the artistic frame of mind: holding onto the primary importance of the sensory world and secondarily worrying about the verbal world. You are
not really working as an actor, however, until you become part of

the collaborative ensemble. This means you must face the literature squarely and learn to fulfill the playwright's intentions without losing the creative state of mind.

In this chapter you will approach the performance of a monologue using the playwright's words and creating the playwright's given circumstances. You will use the techniques you have previously practiced, adding a few new twists to preserve your actor's frame of mind.

---

performance exercise

monologue

This exercise requires a prepared monologue, one to two minutes long, memorized in advance. (Advice on how to choose and memorize monologues appears at the end of the book in the Resources section.) This could be the same material you used for the exercises in Chapter 7.

Use whatever props and furniture you need to simulate the proper environment. It's customary to keep these to a minimum when performing extracted monologues, but for this exercise it is better not to mime. Supply the objects you must use during the piece.

Read the following material on how to introduce and end your presentation. When performing your monologue, concentrate more heavily on the sensory world suggested by the playwright than on how the piece will sound and look. (It will be helpful to videotape your performance. You will not be consulting this tape for some time, and you are not performing for the camera. You are just taping the monologue for future reference.) *Before doing the exercise, read the following discussion.*

Theoretically, this exercise should be as easy to perform as previous ones (the everyday task, for example), but we know this isn't so. Though you are calling the same abilities into play, the situation has changed in one fundamental way: the impetus is no longer your imagination, but a script. This detail changes the picture considerably, so much so that many students temporarily regress when they attempt this exercise. To see why, we need only make a couple of observations about the nature of scripts.

Unlike your imagination, which is very deep, complex, and divergent, a script is a finite and ordered thing. It is a symbolic creation, made up (at least on the surface) of our most potent symbols—words. The problem is not that we think shallowly about these words, but that it is initially difficult to see how to explore them in any other way than by experimenting with how to say them. For this reason, many students who have given detailed, fascinating performances of previous exercises suddenly revert to extremely symbolic performances of their scripts in this exercise.

The following hints have been developed and employed by professional actors to get them over this hurdle. There is no deep mystery to them. They are simply *rehearsal,* those practices normally used to prepare a performance. This is not the only way to rehearse, but only one suggested method to get you started. As you gain experience, you may find ways to modify it to suit your own style better. Until you know your personal instrument better, however, this is a protocol on which you can rely.

Step 1: Select Material
Using the guidelines on selecting a monologue from the Resources section, or alternatively using guidelines issued by your classroom instructor, choose a monologue to perform for this exercise. Clarify in advance with instructors whether this may be material you have used before in your current class or in previous work. Many professors believe that old material brings with it old (bad) habits and prefer you choose material that you have not previously performed. Be personally wary of any material that is associated in your mind with someone else's performance. Monologues from films, for example, are notoriously difficult to perform because you so often end up consciously or unconsciously imitating the original performance.

Step 2: Explore
Do not rush to settle on a final performance. Explore! A sign of potential in a young actor is the ability to be patient. Studies have shown that artists of all kinds have a very high tolerance for ambiguity. They are willing to allow an answer to emerge slowly rather than force it. Read your script carefully, several times, but do not worry about how you will perform it or how it should sound. Read it for its possibilities. Pay careful attention to any details that will help you understand the given circumstances. Look not only at the stage directions but at the speeches for clues to the environment imagined by the playwright. Don't settle for the immediate and obvious. Don't

assume that all the clues will be direct statements of fact like *Boy, it's hot today!* A clever playwright finds many indirect ways of making the point.

Once you have had time to evaluate the script, mock up a little space that can serve as the imaginary place in which your monologue is set. If your setting is in a living room, pull up a couple of chairs and see if you can find something to serve as a coffee table.

Explore the space, the imaginary environment, just as you would explore a sensory object. Treat it as one large sensory exploration exercise. You are not using any words. Just discover this place with your senses.

It is common for people attempting this exercise, after undertaking this exploration for a minute or two, to suddenly recognize this activity: it is *play,* just like they did as children. For some, this is a wonderful release and they dive in wholeheartedly. For many more, this discovery is frightening. They find themselves doing something they deem "childish" and beneath them. They are worried about what others will think of their behavior. Just as you did in the initial sensory exploration exercises, treat these fears as an interfering voice. Don't try to silence the voice, but don't obey it either. Simply continue your work. The exploration may take as long as an hour. It may take place in a real environment, such as a park, or be mocked up on a stage. It doesn't matter how you do it, but it's important that you impress the life of the play on your senses before you try to perform the words.

Then, or perhaps at a later rehearsal where you have warmed up and done an abbreviated sensory exploration, begin to speak while living in this world. Be careful not to slip into a "performance," but instead try out a phrase here and there. Don't worry if you mumble or get lost or any number of unprofessional things. You are just pretending. Speak while holding on to a given circumstance. Let the spirit of play fill you. Some actors find it helpful to paraphrase for a while, others improvise lines that are possible in this world but are not necessarily those of the play.

> *As we were working on a scene, I was talking to myself. "Oh! Oh! That makes me want to . . . Okay . . . ," and I would figure out where their line put me, and then I would respond. Maybe I would respond three or four times, say the same line three of four times as a way of figuring out where it was coming from: "No, that really wasn't it . . . No, that wasn't it either . . . It's this!"*
> *—Stephen Spinella*

Pay particular attention to what the play says you are doing, and do it. If the script indicates you are making a drink, then make one. Let it be much more important than anything you say. Try things many different ways.

Only after a very long time, say a couple of hours (perhaps spread out over a number of rehearsals), should you begin to settle on the form of your final performance. Even that should remain as loose as possible. It may be important that you confine your movement to a particular area, or that you cross to a prop on a particular line. Do what must be done, of course, but be very careful about getting so specific that you have planned gestures and inflections. It is most important that you remain in the creative state of mind. You have had enough experience with it to recognize it by feel. Now is the time to be extraordinarily careful that you work within it.

> *Learn the role, not the lines.*
> *—Tony Barr*

Step 3: Memorize

Only after you have taken the time to explore the physical life of the piece thoroughly should you begin to memorize it. For many beginners, this is surprising.

Memorization is not nearly as difficult as most learners think it will be and should not be the top priority many make it. If you have spent a couple of hours just exploring your piece, you may find you already know it. Try setting your book aside and seeing what you have learned without any particular effort.

If you haven't learned the speech through this method, a little bit of study is in order. Throw away all the techniques you have ever used for learning dates and facts, however, as they won't help you with stage work. Those techniques are designed to put discrete bits of information into your short-term memory. You want to put a sustained passage into your long-term memory. You'll need to work in short, intense bursts combined with physical activity.

Only work about five minutes at a time, on a short passage— say one paragraph. If the script says you are doing something while saying this section, do it while you learn the words. They will be indelibly etched into your mind along with the action.

If there is no action, get up and pace or do some household chore. Lines learned while in motion stick much better than ones you have tried to force into your head while sitting still.

After five minutes of intense work, do something else. Come back to line study when you are fresh. Begin with the section you already know. Say it through to the place at which you stopped, combining it with the action you were doing while you learned it. It will come back. Then add another short section.

Five short bursts of this type, less than a half hour's total work, will be plenty to learn the entire monologue. An hour or more of conventional study may not get you as far.

The biggest problem with lines, by the way, is not learning the words; it is knowing which words come next. Pay attention to the unspoken thoughts that connect each line to the next. If you learn the links between lines you will eliminate the most common memory problem.

Step 4: Create the Combination Performance

After this preparatory period—and only then—you are ready to perform for others. Try not to focus on what they will think, but on your sensory reality. Really live. It is not disrespect but supreme respect for the playwright to remember that the words will mostly take care of themselves. They are the playwright's contribution to the collaboration. Your job is to create the life that accompanies them. You are a collaborator by virtue of your ability to give context to the playwright's meaning. Be confident. Break a leg. Remember to introduce your piece and to end it with the announcement, "Curtain."

Perform the exercise now, before reading further.

Student Portraits

Robert

Robert is tall, lanky, and extremely exuberant. He is a favorite among the group. He has just finished performing his first monologue. His piece is about a young man relating his discovery, through a chance encounter with an "ugly" girl, that he is more excited by intellectual depth than physical beauty.

Robert obviously likes this piece, for a variety of reasons, one of them being that it is liberally sprinkled with profanity with which he hoped to shock the group a bit. Unfortunately, however, the performance has not gone as he hoped. Both he and the group are disappointed in it. Robert walked to the front of the room, turned to face the gang, and spoke intelligently and sincerely, but the piece was strikingly untheatrical and dull.

His classmates immediately say that perhaps they are judging it unfairly. Robert is the class clown and everyone had hoped he would deliver something energetic. What he did deliver was not bad, but it was less interesting than Robert himself.

"It was like Robert giving a book report," Carolyn comments. The instructor agrees. It is not that Robert's friends are not support-ive, but everyone senses there is more there—Robert included.

All are struck by the lack of a sense of place. "Where is this piece set?" the instructor asks Robert. "Well," he says, "I think it is in a bar," and then adds, "but I don't think that has anything to do with what the piece is about." For the moment, the instructor agrees. This character is relating a past experience. The bar does not seem to be a significant detail. Still, it is what the script says. For no other rea-son, the group agrees to mock up a bar setting and have Robert try the piece again. It takes a bit of experimenting. Robert doesn't like the chair Donald has pulled up for him. Deborah finds a stool that gives Robert a greater sense of place. Lawanda offers him a glass she brought in for her monologue. The instructor encourages Robert to use it; drinking certainly seems a logical choice for a bar.

For some reason, though, Robert does not want the drink. "I just don't think I'd want to be getting drunk just now," he says.

"But you're in a bar," Amy says.

"It's where my friends are. I'm here to talk, not drink."

"Good," the instructor says, trying to pursue Robert's line of thought, "but you're still in a bar. Can you be here and not buy a drink?"

"Maybe I'd buy a soft drink or something."

Peter has an empty Coke can, which Robert takes. Suddenly he is transformed. Everyone notices it immediately. There is something in the way he handles the can and seats himself on the stool. He is in a bar and seems unaware of them. They can tell by his behavior.

The instructor quietly urges Robert to do the piece again. He does, and it is as different from his first attempt as can be imagined. Among other things, it is almost embarrassingly personal. He is slightly furtive, speaking in a way that would be acceptable in a bar but trying not to attract attention. The profanity, which popped out the first time, now is a way of keeping the story from seeming sentimental to his friends. Robert seems abashed by what he is saying and roughs it up a bit to keep it from looking silly. The class recognizes that Robert knows whereof he speaks. Robert feels precisely like his character does about intellect being physically exciting, a remarkably private revelation he had hidden from them in his first performance.

The first time around the character seemed so much less interesting than Robert. Now Robert *is* the character, and he is more interesting than anyone had previously imagined. Robert himself explains what he learned. "I didn't think the setting was important, and in a way it wasn't. But as soon as I was sure where I was, it began to affect how I did everything. It is not that I had to, quote, show, unquote, I was in a bar, but being in a bar added so many layers to what I was thinking and doing."

The others in the group congratulate him. The performance was exciting, and they were able to see exactly how the combination of sensory context and script brought it about.

Susan

Susan is very well prepared. Her piece is a young woman talking about her mother. Susan brings lots of props. She busily prepares her scene and performs it with energy and verve. It is pretty good. It still sounds a little stilted, however, and the instructor suggests that she do it again, to see if she can loosen it up. She performs again. It is *exactly* the same. Every movement, every inflection, every pause is the same. It is still good, but still stilted.

The instructor asks Susan to change the action. She does, but the monologue sounds exactly the same. Now she sweeps where formerly she dried dishes, but each gesture is exactly the same length as before.

The group talks about it for a minute. Susan says straightforwardly that she is sure how the monologue should sound and that she wants to make it sound that way. It is a "speech." She is bothered that her instructor wants to change it.

He persists. He talks her into trying an experiment. "Let's see what happens if you don't worry about the sound at all, but really worry about the job." He asks her to sweep the stage. Getting the stage clean is all he cares about for now. Susan tries, but she is almost incapable of doing it. Everyone laughs because the sweeping is so bad. Susan's mind is obviously on the words.

The instructor finally persuades Susan that the sweeping is important too. It is not just a decoration added onto the speech, it is the life of the character. He doubts she will really do it, but she surprises him. Now on her fifth try, she puts her heart into the sweeping. She is determined that the class will not laugh again. They don't. The speech comes out very differently, much more meaningfully than before. Susan is only concentrating on the job, but the words have a new life that is refreshingly honest. It is not "dramatic," as she wanted it to be, but heartfelt and simple. She is much better this way. Everyone sees it immediately.

"Oh, I see," Susan says, "it is not just that you do things, but that you *feel* them." For the first time she grasps the idea of working sensorially.

James

James is frightened. He has done very good work in the preliminary exercises, but he is obviously nervous about doing his monologue. He has put it off as long as possible, and now is sitting white-knuckled on the stage, seemingly unable to begin.

His friends are respectful but surprised. James is a jock. He does not fit the stereotype of the nervous beginner. They silently note that you can never predict who will perform easily and who will get nervous.

It is an act of discipline, but James knows the steps he should take to get himself ready. He introduces his piece, a cutting from a very literate contemporary novel. Then he seats himself and begins to sensorially examine his mocked-up set. His hands shake at first. Slowly, however, he is drawn in. He begins to concentrate; it is like watching someone being hypnotized. He gets calmer and regains his color, and then, before he speaks, he begins a physical transformation. He settles into the chair and looks much older and more confident. He mocks lighting a cigar that he brought as a prop, leans back in the chair, and suddenly looks like a small-town sheriff. He starts to speak. The group barely recognizes the voice. It is a deep growl. James is not putting on a funny voice, he is simply so relaxed that his throat has opened and sound pours out. He has become the character, a man much older and more powerful than the James we know. He is terrific.

Afterward, he can barely remember what he did. The others in the class praise him enthusiastically, but he is unaware of the details they pick out as their favorite moments. He says he only thought about where he was and what he was feeling sensorially. He does not even remember saying some of the lines, let alone how he said them.

James is a good example. His experience is not uncommon. He was nervous while he was preparing, but once he began to perform he was drawn deeply into his inner resources and lost both his fears and his self-consciousness. He predicts (and it turns out to be true) that he will be less nervous next time. He sees now what a different mode of thinking can do.

The class is euphoric at the end of this section of their work. Every person in the group has shown remarkable growth. They have successfully learned to stack the first two layers of their mental abilities. In a stage environment they can create and hold on to a sensory reality while delivering the text of a play, often with surprising results. They see that they have layers of resources of which they were not aware. They are truly beginning to see that acting is a different way of thinking, and that they are mastering it.

They are ready for the next challenge. The next step is to move on from solo work to group work, to scene study with partners, as soon as they have explored the social layer of thinking.

Viewing the Earlier Videotape

If, as suggested in Chapter 1, you made a videotape of yourself performing a speech from a play, watch it now. The purpose of this is not to criticize it or make fun of it. It is to note what you know how to do now that you didn't then. You can expect the performance on the tape to seem rather naïve. It will probably be strongly symbolic and lacking in physicality. Don't demean yourself for not knowing then what you know now. Celebrate your growth.

Don't watch the videotape of your performance of the monologue exercise in this chapter. It is not usually helpful to watch performances immediately afterward. Later, this tape will be helpful. For now, focus only on the old tape, and what you have learned since it was made. This is not a comparative exercise.

Journal Entry: New Skills

In your journal, make notes about the skills you have gained since you began working on the exercises in this book. List the things you did not know how to do.

Now is a good time to begin to measure your artistic progress. Notice your ability to control the creative state. Can you enter it reliably and consciously? How did you master this important skill? Remember what it was like not to know. For fun, try to perform badly. See if you can set up conditions where you do not enter the creative state, do not sense your environment, do not keep the words from taking control. See if you can consciously choose to perform incorrectly. Make notes about this experience.

See if you can identify what new skills you have that prevent you from doing this all the time. Does doing a "bad" performance teach you anything about how you do a good one? Write down your observations.

PARTNER WORK

9 Acting as Interacting

$\int$ ince its historical beginnings twenty-five centuries ago (or more), theatre has been a great communal art. Part of its beauty as it examines the human condition and social experience is that it is a cooperative endeavor. Only rarely do actors perform in solo shows, and even then the actor has almost always had creative partnerships with writers, directors, and designers.

Theatre is a group effort. Actors are part of a creative ensemble, a team. As with any team, the accomplishment of such a collective can be far greater than one person could achieve alone. A powerful group creation can be personally satisfying and artistically extraordinary. For many actors, the most rewarding part of their work is their interrelationships with other performers.

Revisiting the Thought Pyramid

The first part of this book concentrated on the bottom level of the pyramid of thought, sensory awareness. This chapter deals primarily with the second level of the pyramid, social interaction. Human communication is far more than verbal interaction. It is even more than the symbolic gestures through which we attempt to pass infor-

Figure 9.1. Theatre is a group effort. Actors are part of a creative ensemble, a team.

mation to one another. Social interaction is a complex aspect of human behavior and deserves our special consideration.

The Harvard psychologist Howard Gardner has become nationally recognized for his theory that there is more than one form of human intelligence. In his book *Frames of Mind,* Gardner posits that there are seven or more kinds of intelligence. They include logical-mathematical abilities and linguistic abilities (the kind of thing IQ tests usually measure) but also musical, spatial, and athletic abilities. Of particular interest to actors are Gardner's final categories: the personal ones. Intrapersonal intelligence is knowing oneself well—emotional and mental health. Interpersonal intelligence is the ability to know, understand, and interact with others skillfully and consistently.

"These intelligences amount to information-processing capacities—one directed inward, the other outward—which are available to every human infant as part of its species birthright," says Gardner. Our experiences with the exercises in Part 2 helped us discover the truth of this proposition for inwardly directed intelligence. Our specific sensory-perceptual way of thinking (the creative state) is the key to finding our personal creativity.

The exercises in this third part of the book expand our creative state from intrapersonal to interpersonal. In this chapter, we'll find our way into the second realm of our thought pyramid—the social world.

partner exercise 1

see and be seen

This exercise requires a partner and will take about ten minutes. As in previous exercises, set a timer or have someone else keep track of the time for you. The exercise is performed silently. Do not speak.

1. Facing a partner, stand just out of each other's reach, about a yard apart. Stand with your weight squarely on both feet. Let your hands hang loosely at your sides. Do not put them behind your back or in your pockets. Once you begin the exercise, do not adjust your stance or appearance.
2. Just look at each other. Note any desire to speak, to look away, or especially to laugh, but don't do any of these things.
3. Think of your partner as a sensory object. Examine his or her face millimeter by millimeter. Look carefully at his or her features. As much as possible, merely take in the sensory detail as you did with inanimate objects in earlier exercises.
4. Check to see that you are remaining relaxed: your knees should not lock, your breathing should be regular, and your hands should hang loosely by your side.
5. After three or four minutes of studying your partner, turn your gaze away and see if you can visually reconstruct his or her appearance.
6. If time allows and other partners are available, change partners, being particularly careful not to speak, since speaking

will throw you back into logical mode and slow your
progress. (A glance or a nod will be enough to signal a new
partner.)
7. Repeat the exercise.

Do the exercise now, before reading further.

In theory this exercise is just a repetition of earlier work. It is a purely
visual exploration of an object. In practice, however, the fact that the
object is a person changes everything.

You may well have found the exercise difficult. Most people
attempting it for the first time do. Your hands suddenly take on a
life of their own, adjusting your hair more times than you dreamed
possible. You want to giggle or speak. You become self-conscious
looking at your partner, and are very aware that she or he is looking back at you. The soft drink can never did that!

Why is our response so different when dealing with living partners than it is when dealing with objects, even though the process
is almost the same?

The exercise asks us to see and be seen, nothing more. We, however, bring to it a lifetime of dealing with other people that tells us
not to stare, not to intrude, and not to engage anyone too fully. We
look intently only at our most intimate acquaintances.

You may never before have been consciously aware of how
much energy goes into mediating your social interactions, but this
exercise should make you so.

When looking at your partner, you were probably intensely
aware that this was unusual. We rarely stare at people, and we use
numerous signals to tell them not to be threatened when we must
do so. We glance away frequently. We adjust our appearance or otherwise engage our hands in pursuits that clearly do not project any
danger. Sometimes we put our hands in our pockets where they are
completely out of commission. We smile and make small talk. We
do not just see and be seen.

This exercise asked you to transcend normal social boundaries
for a short time. Were you able to let your hands hang quietly at your
side? Could you maintain the silence? Were you able to keep a
"straight face"? Did you or your partner break out laughing, or did
you two smile broadly at one another?

Now think for a moment about the process of the sensory work.
Did looking at the face as an object help you settle down and feel

less self-conscious? How long did it take you compared with the time it took to change to a sensory mode when you explored inanimate objects?

One Act at a Time

There is an old saying in the theatre that you can only put on one act at a time. Just as our old sensory habits can impede our artistic work, so can our old patterns of interacting with others. Just as we had to learn to avoid those old sensory patterns, we have to learn to evade some of our automatic social responses.

Before you can meaningfully engage partners in a scene, you will have to learn to turn off your usual signal systems that tell them you are not staring at them, you are not going to hurt them, and you do not want a deeper interaction with them. This doesn't mean that you are going to hurt them or are starting some complex relationship. It's just that we cannot put on the social act and the artistic act simultaneously. We have to leave behind some of the social habits that signal separation and distance before we can assume the intense interactions of the stage.

Student Portraits

Kim and Marcus pair up, and like others in the room, they cheerfully ignore the instruction not to talk. Partner work has finally arrived and they are laughing and joking. Everyone in the class is in a similar mood, so it's a bit of a surprise when the instructor very firmly asks that everyone turn and *silently* face his or her partner.

The group soon settles into a quiet, uncomfortable silence. Nearly everyone is having difficulty doing the exercise. The instructor quietly asks the class to check to see that their knees are not locked, that they are not holding their breath, that their hands are relaxed and not made into fists, and that they are not adjusting their appearance. As soon as he finishes the checklist, he has to begin again. While checking for locked knees, many unconsciously clench their fists. When relaxing their fists, they hold their breath.

Kim is having more difficulty than anyone. She bursts out giggling whenever she so much as glances at Marcus. He is stoic at first, but the longer the exercise goes on the more he, too, breaks into laughter.

Kim finally looks at the floor, and Marcus regains control. The instructor gently tells them that laughter is a choice they are making in order to avoid the contact. Kim says she is sorry, but that she "can't control it." Again the instructor asserts, firmly but not angrily, that they *can* control it, particularly if they hasten the switch to the alternate mental state by concentrating on each other's face like a sensory object. Both seem a little chastened, but they do improve.

Slowly, Kim, Marcus, and the others begin to find a bit more comfort, but it is a good five minutes before the room settles down. Many still unconsciously smooth their hair, straighten their clothing, and shift their stance, at regular intervals. After about ten minutes, during which no one has really succeeded at the exercise, the group changes partners.

For a very brief moment things are even worse, but this time comfort settles in much faster. Marcus is noticeably more at ease with his second partner and settles into something that looks a bit like a trance as he stares at his new partner. Kim is still uncomfortable, but not nearly so much as she had been with Marcus.

This round, more of the group find a way to settle into their alternate mental states more quickly. The self-consciousness fades faster. Soon the whole room is quietly just seeing and being seen.

The description of the exercise had seemed so easy. The group is genuinely astonished at how hard this simple-sounding exercise proved to be. Talking about it later, Kim says that she could feel herself being overwhelmed by discomfort but that she did learn to recognize when she was choosing to break the tension by laughing or moving or, especially, looking away. For her, today has been about learning to ride out the discomfort until she was able to make the switch to the sensory way of thinking. At that point, she was able to complete the work.

partner exercise 2

see and be seen 2

In this exercise, you will observe personality as well as appearance. Again, it will take about ten minutes. As before, set a timer or have someone else keep track of the time for you. Do not speak.

1. Stand facing your partner, just out of each other's reach, about a yard apart, your weight squarely on both feet, your arms hanging loosely at your sides.
2. Precisely as you did in the first exercise, look at your partner and begin to think of her or him as a sensory object.
3. Examine her or his face millimeter by millimeter. Look carefully at the facial features.
4. Check to see that you are staying relaxed: your knees should not lock, your breathing should be regular, and your hands should hang loosely by your sides.
5. As you look at your partner, see what you can deduce about her or his personality. What makes this person happy? Can you tell by looking? What makes her or him angry or sad?
6. Think about your partner as someone capable of great tenderness. What clues in her or his appearance tell you how she or he would show this tenderness? Would he envelop you in a big bear hug? Would she leave a quiet, anonymous note? Now think about her or him as capable of great violence. (Though we don't like to acknowledge it, violence is a possibility in anyone). How would she or he express this violence when pushed to the extreme? Would she savagely attack? Would he stealthily and quietly get revenge? This should not be idle speculation. Deduce the possibilities from the way your partner looks.
7. If there is time, change partners and do the exercise again.

Do the exercise now, before reading further.

By now you are probably becoming more accustomed to working with another person. After even a couple of repetitions, some of the self-consciousness of the interaction begins to fade away. You can take in more than you could in your first tries. Good! It is a particular kind of acting skill to be able to set aside social habit and really look at a partner without using the usual filters.

It is, literally, a kind of intelligence to begin to sense who your partner is from subtle signals in his or her appearance and behavior. This level of the exercise may have again made you uncomfortable, however. For many students it is quite difficult to image their partner as angry or violent. Anyone *can* become violent, but we don't always want to acknowledge that potential. Tenderness and nurturing are more acceptable social acts, but even they can make us uncomfortable. It is hard to separate the potential of our partner to be tender from imagining him or her in a personal relationship with us.

Before we can meaningfully interact with other actors on the stage, we have to accept the full range of their potential. Plays are full of interactions of the richest and most exciting kind. Theatrical relationships often deal with matters of utmost importance—with life and death. Hamlet avenges his father; Medea kills her children to avenge her husband's betrayal. Even the most mundane naturalism is filled with interpersonal intensity. If we cannot accept our partner's potential to express those emotions, our performance will remain superficial and symbolic. Our acting will subtly—or not so subtly—signal the audience, *This is not me. I am not really here. This is not real.*

There are two ways to leap this hurdle.

The first is to develop a theatrical mindset within which to work. It may be difficult when you first interact with a partner to know with whom you are working: a person, an actor, a character, or some combination of all of them? Of course your partner is both a person and an actor, but within the context of any theatrical exercise, your partner is always a *character.* The relationship you develop, the potential you acknowledge, the reality you recognize, has boundaries. Othello can kill you, but only within the world of the play. John is your friend. Your relationship to his Othello is not the same as your relationship to him. Making this important distinction will enable you to drop many of the social conventions that prevent true interaction. You must seek out and acknowledge the real potential of your partner to have behavioral extremes that can include both violence and nurturing, and at the same time engage this reality only within the theatrical context.

The second way is to engage your partner as you did in the sensory objects in Chapter 4. This acknowledges his or her physical reality in the here and now. At the same time, because it emanates from the wholistic processes of the brain rather then the sequential ones, it avoids the logical tangles that sequential processing creates.

Creating a Relationship

Having found a neutral place from which to interact with your partner, it is possible to begin to engage him or her in a more theatrical way. Seeing and being seen, however interesting to the participants, is not very engaging to watch.

Discovering and creating relationships is a central part of the actor's art. It is the active embodiment of contact and communication. It requires that you start with a personal openness, uncluttered by old social habits. It progresses through your active attempts to influence your fellow actors. The following exercise explores this phenomenon.

> **relationship exercise**
>
> **changing your partner's behavior**

This exercise will take about ten minutes. As in previous exercises, set a timer or have someone else keep track of the time for you.

1. Find a place to work where you and your partner have room to move about somewhat without running into other people or objects. Stand facing each other, about an arm's length apart.
2. Begin as you did the previous exercise, just seeing and being seen. Allow yourself to settle into the exercise. Wait until you feel your concentration (in the alternate mental state) kick in.
3. Now, without touching or speaking to your partner, see if you can influence your partner's behavior. Try to make her smile. Or see if you can startle him. Think about influencing her to move a step closer. Or try to repel him so that he physically moves away. Decide in advance what you want to accomplish and see if you can change your partner's behavior.

Do the exercise now, before reading further.

Were you able to alter your partner's behavior? Did your partner alter yours? Because your partner was aware of the goal of the exercise, he may have been very guarded, but this exercise succeeds more often than it fails. At the same time, it is common to indicate to your partner what you want her to do, rather than take an action that alters her behavior. It may take an attempt or two to see what is required to create a real change in your partner's behavior.

Student Portrait

Sam

Several pairs of students are working together as the class attempts the changing-your-partner's-behavior exercise. Paul is making faces at Deborah, hoping to make her laugh, but she is fully aware of his goal; he becomes embarrassed when she refuses to crack even the smallest smile. He is going to have to work much harder, and more cleverly, in order to change her demeanor. Elsewhere in the room, Karen is crooking her first finger at Tom. It is a blatant signal, one we use all the time in life, but Tom does not approach her. It is not a compelling action. Suddenly Sam, who has been jumping around and acting silly to amuse Susan, stumbles and falls. He is lying on the floor grasping his ankle and moaning. The entire exercise is disrupted and nearly everyone in the room is gathering around him to see if he is badly hurt. The instructor parts the crowd in order to reach him, when Sam suddenly looks up and smiles broadly. "I think I understand the exercise," he says as he stands up, obviously uninjured. A murmur of consternation sweeps the room, but soon the group sees he is right. He *does* understand the exercise. Most pairs have adopted strategies that openly announce themselves as artificial. They are "acts." Making faces and acting silly sometimes elicited a smile or a giggle, but more often they were seen as tricks. Sam, however, attempted to get his partner to touch him by feigning an accident. His partner didn't suspect, nor did anyone else in the room, that this behavior was an acting strategy. It seemed real. An observer or two suggests that Sam was cheating. Susan, in particular, is incensed that he would deliberately mislead the group. Sam, however, has done what was asked for within the context of the exercise. The action outside on the sidewalk might be manipulative, but here he was doing something to genuinely change his partner's behavior.

Eventually, even Susan becomes philosophical about Sam's action. "How do you know what is real and what isn't?" she asks. She is a little surprised when her instructor says that acting *is* real. It occurs within the theatrical context of the stage, but in all other ways it is real human interaction. Oddly enough, it is life that is sometimes *unreal*. In everyday social encounters we often use elaborate social signals to pretend the situation is not what we all know it to be. The signals we identified in the see-and-be-seen exercise

Figure 9.2. Acting comes alive when you know your actions are changing your partner's behavior.

function to defuse the intense reality of the situation. We pretend that standing so close and staring is neither disconcerting nor dangerous. Our signals say, *This is not an intense experience,* when we all know that it is!

> *This is the very essence of acting—action and response. In other words, I attempt something and in that moment I have to be very receptive to your response, which will, in turn, become a reaction in me. All training leads to this. . . . It's like fishing. The fisherman and the fish go together.*
> —Warren Robertson

Sam, admittedly a bit melodramatically, suddenly saw through the superficial layer of pretended behavior and found a way to create a real change in Susan. Lacking subtlety, he had changed everyone else's partner as well, but the lesson was interesting for all. The response was real instead of a preplanned and mutually arranged "deal." At first, Susan felt manipulated. She wanted to be warned. She wanted a layer of artificiality that would protect her feelings from being engaged. She confessed later that what she had wanted at the time *was* a symbolic interaction. The reality of Sam's tactic had disturbed her. But it had worked, more effectively than anything else tried by anyone.

We learned this same lesson at the sensory level, but now we have learned it at the social level. Acting requires the real engagement of our senses, not the superficial symbolic summary we mentally depend on most of the time. Likewise, interacting with another person requires dropping symbolically managed superficial exchanges and moving to a level of genuine exchange.

Journal Entry: Partner Work

In your journal, enter your observations about working with partners. Detail the work you did, to remind yourself of the partners you worked with and your initial reactions. Write down any observations you had about the nature of your interactions. Were you able to see and be seen? Were you comfortable observing personality, having your personality observed? Were you able to change your partner's behavior? Did yours change in response to your partner? What did you like and dislike about the experience?

Related Optional Exercises

1. Stand facing a partner, about an arm's length apart. Let one partner initiate a series of small movements that the other

partner will try to mirror perfectly and simultaneously, as if he or she is the reflection of the first person. Concentrate on getting the detail of the movement right. After a few minutes, let the follower become the leader.

2. Stand facing a partner as in the previous exercise, but with a hand behind your back so that your partner can't see it. Do the see-and-be-seen exercise, but imagine that you have a dagger in your hand. See how this affects your relationship. Imagine instead that you have a bouquet of flowers. Does this change your relationship? Imagine that you have a gun, a snake, a hundred-dollar bill. Mix them up so your partner does not know the order of your imaginings. See if he can detect any changes in you. Change roles, so that your partner has the imaginary objects behind his back. See if you notice any difference in his demeanor and attitude as the imaginary objects change.

3. Using a prop telephone, imagine a conversation with some-one you know very well. Carry on your part of the conversa-tion. Listen for, and actually hear, the voice of the person to whom you are speaking. Choose someone you know well enough to predict what she would say. Create the sensation of her voice. Hear the sound of her inflections. Concentrate only on sensations.

Choice

In a theatre in Washington, D.C., Tom Hulce (most famous for play-ing Mozart in the film *Amadeus*) is performing the role of Hamlet. Midway through his first scene, the ghost of Hamlet's father appears and summons Hamlet to him. The color drains from Hulce's face. Stunned, he falls to his knees and listens, and then, as the apparition speaks, he crawls across the floor and reaches out to it. His hand unexpectedly hits something solid and his paleness dis-appears. Where I am sitting, near the stage, I can see the blood rush to Hulce's cheeks. He is shocked that his dead father is so real and tangible. I can practically hear his heart pounding. It is an intensely moving performance. All the character's grief and longing for his father are dispelled by one moment of contact with him. His pur-pose never wavers from that moment in the play.

What I saw, I learned later, was Hulce's thirtieth or so perform-ance of the role. It had been wonderfully moving, so I was surprised when I also discovered that Hulce had been fighting off a cold at the time. That performance had been particularly difficult for him. He had had trouble maintaining his energy.

I never suspected. Hulce's actions seemed so fresh and spontaneous that I believed "the illusion of the first time." I thought I might have seen a particularly intense performance. But people connected with the show confirmed that he performed this scene this way, complete with noticeable blanching and, later, visible flushing, every night.

One might well wonder how Hulce was able to find such spontaneity and commitment in each and every performance. It was hardly a surprise that the ghost would appear; the cast had rehearsed the play for weeks. It was even less of a surprise that the ghost was "solid." A flesh-and-blood actor was playing the role.

Within the world of the play, however, Hulce managed to repeat actions every night with firmness of conviction and believability. He chose a series of actions each night with a freshness that made them seem to be happening for the first time.

This skill is closely related to the abilities we have been exploring. At first, it may seem to be the opposite of what we explored in Chapter 9. There we learned something about behaving truthfully in spontaneous circumstances. Here the problem is creating an *illusion* of spontaneity. (Remember the punch line, "Sincerity is everything. If you can fake that, you got it made"?)

The underlying skill, however, is not one of faking anything. Just as we originally learned to engage our senses fully, then to interact with a partner realistically, now we will see that the illusion of the first time derives from the ability to *choose* our actions fully each time we do them, even in highly rehearsed and scripted situations.

The following exercise will help you learn to experience your choices fully, not just mindlessly repeat your actions, even in situations that impose many obstacles.

choice exercise 1

sixteen steps

From available furniture, create a simple environment. You'll need an entrance, one or more places to sit, and a place to set things down. The exercise requires five participants: four actors and a monitor. Before the exercise begins, each actor needs to come up with two lines to speak in the course of the scene. These lines are arbitrary and up to the performer. They may be quotes, everyday phrases, or made up.

As the scene begins, actor A is seated, actors B and C are standing, and actor D is waiting just outside the entrance. There are sixteen clearly delineated steps in the exercise:

Step 1: B speaks his first line.

Step 2: D knocks on the door.

Step 3: A says her first line.

Step 4: C crosses to the door.

Step 5: C opens the door.

Step 6: D enters and speaks his first line.

Step 7: C responds with her first line.

Step 8: All choose to do nothing.

Step 9: B says his second line.

Step 10: D crosses to B.

Step 11: D says his second line.

Step 12: A says her second line.

Step 13: C crosses to A.

Step 14: A stands and exits.

Step 15: B crosses to C.

Step 16: C says her final line.

First you'll need to rehearse the sequence. Walk through the exercise several times, with the monitor calling out the steps. Once everyone has the sequence memorized, the monitor should stop calling out the steps and instead clap once loudly to initiate the action of each step. Each clap represents a point at which one or more of the participants is making a choice to do a prescribed action. Make each step a clearly isolated unit. Pay particular attention to Step 8. Do not skip it or shortchange it. It is a full step in which everyone *chooses* to do nothing.

Now go through the sequence again, but briefly consider not taking the action each time. Consciously choose to do the assigned step, but only after considering *not* doing it.

Throughout the exercise, don't discuss the ramifications of what you are doing with your fellow actors. Keep extraneous talk to a minimum. It is the monitor's job to keep rehearsal on track and to discourage too much discussion. Simply repeat the exercise, with everyone committing themselves to the actions specified in the sixteen steps. However, if something seems to be developing through action (such as a plot or relationship), allow it.

Figure 10.1. Choice is a powerful tool, even in a moment of stillness.

After a time, perhaps at a later session, begin working on a unified scene. Your particular combination of lines, choices, and relationships will probably already have developed into the rudiments of an obvious story. Discuss what seems to be suggested by the scene so far. Come to a consensus so that everyone is working in the same direction.

The next part of the exercise is crucial: begin to strengthen the series of choices that combine to make an intelligible story. Continue to rehearse the scene as a group, but don't discuss what you are doing, with the following exception: you may identify the stimuli leading up to a choice and ask that they be continued and perhaps made more specific. (For example, if a general menacing tone prompts one of your lines, you may ask that the menace be conveyed more strongly.) You may say only what you need, but not how the other actor is to do it.

After you have rehearsed the scene several times, perform it for observers. Allow them to identify the story line. If they cannot, go back into rehearsal and discuss which choices must be made stronger in order to make the story clear.

Do the exercise now, before reading further.

Taking Action Through Choice

Logically, this exercise should become more and more stale each time it is performed. The script's lack of sense should become reinforced. Repeating senselessness should make things worse, shouldn't it? We should be creating a performance that is rote and meaningless, more so with each repetition.

It is astonishing that the opposite, in fact, happens. Through our careful reworking of the series of lines and actions, we find more, not less, sense in the scene. Things that have no connection to each other come together to tell a story. How can this be?

The Danger of the Preordained

The preordained does present dangers to the performer's frame of mind. Like adding speech, being tied to a script confronts us with ideal conditions for slipping back into the step-by-step logic that leads to symbolic performances. But at the same time, unless we work in a company committed to improvisation we are tied to the script. That is the nature of theatre.

We don't have the freedom to change even small details around nightly to help create some small freshness and excitement. The lines must come in the same order. The blocking must remain consistent for the lighting and special effects to work.

> *Some actors have an almost architectural plan for the character. I've always envied this. I not only don't have a grand overall plan, I don't have a pencil. The choices I'm making are of the moment. . . . I work this way: I don't know what's going on in my fellow actor's mind; I'm listening to him; I'm thinking; and I come up with a choice. I start to do it. Maybe I think, No, and begin to go with another choice.*
> *—Dianne Wiest*

In executing the previous exercise we begin to see how to find the special frame of mind that evades the problems of repetition and the preordained. Choice is the mental element that allows us to experience actions freshly and spontaneously each and every time we do them.

This exercise is a way to discover that the ability to meld a series of choices is "acting." Simply by connecting a series of choices, you have created an identifiable character in a scene. In most cases actors find themselves completely transformed in these "mini-performances" into something quite unlike themselves without ever having thought about an external appearance. In fact, characterization is just making the choices the character makes under the specific stimuli of the scene.

The sixteen-steps exercise is an adaptation of the work of Robert Benedetti, one of the best-known American authors on acting. He observes that choice is the tool that brings about the transformation of the actor from puppet to coparticipant with the author in creating the performance. Once you have been through it, you see this is an exercise in "gestalting" all your previous skills into a single unit. You are acting.

Student Portraits

Choosing the lines they will speak has been especially fun for Dan, Sam, Wallace, and Susan. Amy, their monitor, is having a bit of trouble keeping them on task. Clearly they are enjoying thinking of the most ridiculous or incompatible lines. Susan has already decided that she will use a favorite Chekhov line, "I'm in mourning for my life." The fact that the line seems wildly out of context, even in the play it's from, attracts her.

Others are fishing around a bit. Dan wants to use a Molière line in the original French, but when he admits that he can't remember what it means (he just likes the sound of it), the others discourage him. Wallace, ever the joker, comes up with sentences that are grammatically correct but make no sense. "The audible blue is eating his celery" is one of them. Sam is in a Beckett mood and chooses banalities: "I can't go on" and "I'm hungry, I want to eat."

On the whole they are a more literate group than usual. Amy is impatient with their erudition and asks them to get on with it. In the end, the scholarly gives way to the pragmatic and the last few lines are hurriedly assembled. No one yet believes that it will make no difference what the lines mean. They even feel a certain glee in coming up with some lines that so lack sense the exercise *cannot* work. Dan does choose a French phrase, but it is a commonplace of which he and others know the meaning, "Chaque á son gout" [Each to his own taste].

Amy insists they start rehearsal. Susan is actor A. Her two lines are "It's ten o'clock. Do you know where your children are?" and the

Chekhov line. Dan is B. In addition to his French line he has decided on the very heartfelt "I hope to graduate soon." Sam is C, and Wallace is therefore D. For his second line he has chosen the phrase "Just don't push me."

The whole script now looks like this:

Step 1: DAN speaks his first line. "I hope to graduate soon."

Step 2: WALLACE knocks on the door.

Step 3: SUSAN says her first line. "I'm in mourning for my life."

Step 4: SAM crosses to the door.

Step 5: SAM opens the door.

Step 6: WALLACE enters and speaks his first line. "The audible blue is eating his celery."

Step 7: SAM responds with his first line. "I'm hungry, I want to eat."

Step 8: All choose to do nothing.

Step 9: DAN says his second line. "Chaque á son gout." [Each to his own taste.]

Step 10: WALLACE crosses to DAN.

Step 11: WALLACE says his second line. "Just don't push me."

Step 12: SUSAN says her second line. "It's ten o'clock. Do you know where your children are?"

Step 13: SAM crosses to SUSAN.

Step 14: SUSAN stands and exits.

Step 15: DAN crosses to SAM.

Step 16: SAM says his final line. "I can't go on."

They mock up a hasty set consisting of a single chair. The storage closet door becomes the entrance. It takes four repetitions with Amy calling out the steps before everyone feels secure with the sequence. They are walking through the exercise, which is all they are supposed to do.

After the fifth walk-through, Amy no longer calls the steps but just claps her hands sharply to initiate each step. When it is completed, she allows a little pause before clapping again for the next step. At Step 8, when nothing should happen, Dan jumps the gun and says his line. Amy reminds them that Step 8 is a full step in which nothing happens.

The sixth and seventh walk-throughs go smoothly; everyone mechanically performs his or her actions and says the lines. Still, with no one making any effort whatsoever, a couple of relationships and a rudimentary story begin to emerge. The cast is unaware of this, but Amy sees it quite clearly. It is all she can do to keep from blurting out directions.

The first connection in the piece is Sam's responding, "I'm hungry, I want to eat," to Wallace's "The audible blue is eating his celery." It is funny. Wallace delivers his line like a beat poet; Sam, the "dumb guy," clearly doesn't get it, and responds only to the mention of food. It is the first link of cause and effect. Dan's "I hope to graduate soon" elicits Susan's "I'm in mourning for my life," which also becomes a direct response: she has no such hope. Another connection is made.

More bits and pieces begin to emerge. One of the most interesting is the "empty" Step 8. Everyone grinds to a complete halt in reaction to Sam's response to the celery line. They all turn and stare at him. It gets a huge laugh from some kibitzers. Clearly this group's exercise is emerging as a comedy.

The group is now in their tenth or so walk-through, about a half hour into rehearsal. Everyone is beginning to see that *choice* is a kind of glue holding random bits together. "Hearing" something and choosing an action based on what is heard *creates* cause and effect. Lines take on interesting new meanings. Susan's final line, "It's ten o'clock. Do you know where your children are?" doesn't refer to parentage at all. She is sarcastically chiding Wallace for his childishly bullying behavior to both Dan and Sam.

This group's little play has emerged as a twenty-something situation comedy. The characters are quite funny. There is a self-important poet, a sassy girl-next-door, a dumb sidekick, and our hapless hero. The formula is well known. By repetition thirteen or fourteen the piece is a polished and clever parody of a sitcom.

The group is amazed at their own invention. They were initially trying to thwart the exercise by finding completely unrelated (and maybe unrelatable) lines, only to discover that the act of making choices gave their nonsense script a readily discernible story line.

Later, when talking with members of the other groups, they find that not only is this universally true, but so is its opposite—closely related lines don't automatically create stories and relationships until the actors make choices.

Layered Work

Actors who are trained in Stanislavski's methodologies are sometimes criticized for their absolute devotion to sensory work while ignoring larger issues. In this exercise the cast began to see what that criticism is all about, and the grain of truth in it. (Stanislavski never forgot the larger issues, but a few of his followers did.) Sensory work makes the individual moments truthful and lifelike, but choice is required to pull them together into something larger. Sensory work and choice are each part of the actor's arsenal. The following exercise helps sharpen your awareness of this skill. Because it happens in a literary context, you will also begin to see more about how plays are constructed.

choice exercise 2

say no before you say yes

1. Pick a one-minute monologue or section from a scene.
2. List all the actions in the scene. (A simple list could look like this: open door; enter; sit; speak to other character; find and light a cigarette.)
3. Now, play the scene, but before each action, pause to consider doing the opposite. Mentally choose to say no for just a second before you say yes. (Conversely, choose yes for a second before deciding not to do something.) Before opening the door, consider just walking away instead. Perhaps even start to walk away. Then decide to go ahead and open the door. Before entering, consider stopping outside instead. Consider standing instead of sitting. Weigh the possibility of not speaking to the other character. Think about leaving your cigarettes in your pocket, or putting the cigarette back in the pack instead of lighting it.

Do the exercise now, before reading further.

This process invests the scene with new meaning. The actions are not the mindless movements of a robot, but the purposeful behavior of a human being. You are rediscovering the option of *choosing* an action, not just carrying it out because the script tells you to. Of course, you cannot pause your way through a play. This technique for adding new meaningfulness needs to be balanced against letting a scene keep grinding to a halt.

choice exercise 3

say no before you say yes, fast-forward

Repeat the scene, but make the choices silently and quickly. Think and speak at the same time. (The common theatrical direction is to think on the lines, not between them.) Perform the scene without ponderous pauses, but don't eliminate the choices. Make your choices quickly, while you speak. The object is to smooth out the scene. Stage characters think faster than we do in everyday life.

Do the exercise now, before reading further.

The Essence of Life

A commonplace in theatre (I've often invoked it in this book) is, acting should be truthful. It should be organic. The following exercise helps you understand what this terminology means. Theatre is certainly *not* truthful, if by that we mean that the dialogue must come from life and record that which truly happened. Theatre is not documentary.

When we use the terms *truthful* and *organic* about acting, we mean something about the *process*, not the product. We mean that the actions undertaken by the actor follow the natural patterns of thought and behavior in life. Some actors and coaches think that acting should *mimic* natural behavior, create a convincing illusion of it. That is not what I mean.

To be truthful, acting must use the same processes as we use in life, not imitate them. To that end, acting starts at the first level in the thought pyramid, the sensory level. The actor must be fully engaged sensorially, as we are in life (albeit unconsciously most of the time). When onstage with others, the actor must engage in genuine social interaction, the second level of the pyramid. In life we sometimes use symbolic behavior to excuse ourselves from engaging with another person, and without training, we almost always do so in the theatre as well. But truthful acting follows the natural patterns of complete engagement.

Speech plays a smaller role than the sensory perception and social interaction, but is still present. This speech, however, is not the iteration of uninhabited thought but is specifically chosen and fully sensed. That is to say, it does not override or substitute for the two previous levels but joins them.

This is what happens to us all every day. It is *organic*, meaning that it is the normal operation of the organism. Now that we have experienced these levels it is possible to see that they are what we do naturally, but they are not what we are aware of when we behave in the everyday world. Much of this goes on below the level of our consciousness. In the artificial world of the theatre, truthful, organic behavior must be jump-started. It does not just occur.

Choice is the spoon that blends all these ingredients into a smooth batter. It is the essence of life. We choose to engage our senses. We choose to override our social inhibitions. We choose to invest our actions with meaning and causality. In the next chapter, you will learn how to choose the actions themselves, so that the performance is under your control while corresponding with the needs of the play.

Student Portrait

Dan

Dan is working on the say-yes exercise. He has chosen to use a short portion of his monologue. The instructor agrees that this will work fine. Still everyone's ears perk up just a bit when Dan says that this will help him by giving him more control over the material.

The action sequence is very short. It involves entering, taking off a coat, and pouring a drink. These actions are simple and straightforward. It takes Dan only a minute or two to mock up his space and perform the exercise.

His first time through is a bit perfunctory; he says he was just walking through it to rehearse the actions. Repeating the exercise, however, he is very good. He literally enacts his changes of mind. He places his hand on the door, but instead of turning the handle he slowly withdraws it. It is a conscious choice when he replaces it and opens the door. It is a compelling, rather cinematic, moment. His hand tells a whole story.

Entering the room, he starts to slip out of his coat, but we can see the thought cross his mind that he shouldn't be here. He nudges the coat back up over his shoulder and turns to go. We see quite clearly when he convinces himself that he is doing the best thing after all and determinedly takes the coat off and throws it onto a chair. Or almost throws it. Now getting into the exercise, Dan realizes that this might be a separate choice and retrieves the coat in midthrow. He turns to look for the classroom's coat rack, which is often included in mocked-up sets. It is not where he expects it, and he goes ahead and throws the coat on the chair. It is marvelous—quite spontaneous—and illustrates very clearly that Dan understands this exercise.

He goes to the "bar," and starts to pour himself a drink. After a moment's thought he changes his mind and, after replacing the first bottle, takes a different one, from which he pours the drink. He hasn't yet spoken. He is about to say the first line of the monologue, when the instructor stops him. It is a good exercise as is. Dan has clearly performed the task at hand. His choices are so clear and vivid, in marked contrast to his first walk-through, that no comment is necessary.

The instructor immediately urges Dan on to part 2 of the exercise. Although part 1 has achieved its purpose, it's exhibited the corresponding flaws. It is so detailed that each little action has become a story. The alternatives to the choices have become so vivid, the character looks like someone who can't make up his mind, which is not what the script is about. It's time to smooth out the process.

Dan begins again. He executes the door business much more quickly and enters. The instructor interrupts: "The door business was better, but perhaps the choosing could happen entirely in your head."

Back to the beginning. Dan again enters, this time with only the slightest hesitation in his reach. The pause probably would not be noticeable to anyone not watching the action carefully. Dan slips his coat off quickly, not observably hesitating but keeping the midair retrieval of the coat. It is an interesting mix. He is trying to keep the exercise moving, but he's also working at keeping the choices alive. He crosses to make the drink, and starts to repeat the bottle switching. In setting aside the first bottle, however, Dan misjudges its position and it tips over and a bit of the liquid spills out.

Dan makes a time-out gesture. There are napkins on the table, and he puts one or two on the spill. Satisfied, he says, "Okay." He then picks up the first bottle again, starts to pour the drink, changes his mind, switches bottles (this time without incident), and concludes the sequence.

Overall, the exercise is better. The instructor points out that the choices are smooth, clear, detailed. Dan has committed to his actions and they are interesting and fully felt. Dan has learned how to avoid the problems of mindless repetition.

However, a new issue has been raised. All the observers want to discuss the accidental spill, and the instructor concedes that this was indeed the crucial moment in the scene.

Moment-to-Moment Work

Dan's accident is a variation of a common occurrence in the performances of beginning actors, what one master teacher has called the Can-I-start-over? phenomenon.

> Stanislavski's art, his humanism, his great gift to the world theatre, was the recognition that on the stage, just as in the office or the supermarket or the school, human beings must concern themselves with the truth of the individual moment, and recognize and ratify their coconspirator's existence and desire.
> —David Mamet

Things don't always go as planned. Something happens you didn't intend. A line is forgotten or spoken at the wrong time. Props are in unexpected positions. Furniture makes sudden squeaks and groans.

One's first impulse is to ignore the mischance—to cancel it out. Dan did so quite explicitly by signaling a time-out. He didn't want the mistake to be included in an evaluation of his work.

The opposite, however, proved true. It was the moment most recalled by his observers. The curious mixture of symbolic behavior and stepping out of the action made this the most memorable thing Dan did.

Given the danger preordained action and specified words hold relative to the actor's frame of mind, we need to specify some of the implications for performance.

Acting is not repetition in any sense. It is reinvesting in each word, and each action of the play, each time we do it. These principles apply during rehearsals, but also during the real time of performance. Performance is more like an ongoing improvisation within a set of given circumstances than it is like a presentation of the preordained.

Simply put, whatever happens when we perform is part of the performance. Dan's spilled drink is the unexpected moment that so often invades our lives. It happened to Dan, but he didn't want it to happen to his character, so he attempted to exempt it from his watchers' consciousness. That being impossible, he settled for a symbolic gesture that asked our tacit cooperation.

Instead, Dan could have, and should have, incorporated the moment into the performance. Dan's character could have cleaned up the spill as easily as Dan himself (stepping momentarily out of character) did.

Having learned sensorial truthfulness, social truthfulness, and organic verbalization, we must learn to exercise them all in real time. If the furniture squeaks, acknowledge it; react to it.

As a beginning actor, I was part of a performance in which an actor's hat accidentally fell off during the first scene. Everyone in the cast was young. We all knew it was a mistake, but we determinedly ignored it. For the whole first act everyone stepped gingerly over and around it, always careful to block out its presence. How easy it would have been for any of us, at any point, to reach over and pick up the hat. If we saw one lying in the middle of our home, we would do so. (I remember asking a friend later what he had thought of the performance. "The hat was very good," he said.)

What is actually happening must be encompassed as truthfully as what is actually there to be seen, felt, and heard. This is especially true of what our fellow actors do in a scene. In performance we may not like the choices they are making, we may not appreciate their subtle (or overt!) variations from what we have rehearsed. We may be outraged by their paraphrase of a line or their retiming of an action. Off stage your director may agree with you and reprimand them, but in the moment what is, *is*. While performing, you can only react to what is actually said and done—to what occurs. The unplanned and the unexpected must be organically and truthfully incorporated, like everything else.

> *If an actor doesn't do what you think they are supposed to do, you think, They didn't do that right, they should do this. Nine times out of ten, you may be right. So what? You're right, but you're alone.*
> —*Olympia Dukakis*

This combination of skills—sensorially, socially, and linguistically investing truthfully and organically in the performance moment—is the range of abilities employed in acting. Organizing these skills into a form that serves the play is the next step, and the subject of the next chapter.

Journal Entry: Choice Exercises

In your journal write a description of your sixteen-steps exercise. Be sure to include your two lines and the lines of your partners, as you remember them. Try to describe the story that eventually emerged and the key choices that created the cause and effect. Write notes about the process, and the part you played in it.

Think about how choice is related to earlier work on other thought-pyramid levels. Can you explain how it is an echo of the processes invoked there? Is there a common metaphor that all these exercises share?

Related Optional Exercises

1. In a real place—perhaps your room—hide a key or some similar small object. Imagine that you have lost this item. Begin looking for it. Re-create the process of choosing all the sensible places you will look. (Maybe you will look where the item is, and not "find" it.) Think what such a search is really like. Think of a reason why you may search again in some of the places you have already looked. Choose to sit for a second and try to remember where you last had the item. Let an inspiration strike you. Search there. It's not the right spot. Now remember where the item is, and "find" it.

2. Do the exercise again, with higher stakes. Imagine the lost item is a multimillion-dollar winning lottery ticket. Let your fears that you have lost it play on you as you search. Get des-

perate before you remember where you hid the ticket for safe-keeping. Search everywhere. Make choices strong enough to justify looking in wildly unlikely places like in the refrigerator or under items too small to cover the ticket.

3. Do the same set of actions based on three different sets of imaginary circumstances. For example, bring your roommate a present. Imagine that you are angry with him or her, but you want to make up. Then imagine that you are delivering a present to your roommate on behalf of someone else and you want to see what is in it. Finally, imagine that the present is something from a mutual acquaintance that you do not trust. Deliver the present with all the caution a bribe deserves. How do the changing circumstances affect your choices?

11 Steering the Performance

M y character wouldn't do that!" is the punch line of many a theatrical joke. A young actor, committed to pursuing organic
truth, finds himself at the crucial juncture of the play, film, or
teleplay, and refuses to carry out the required action. It is such a
cliché that few outside the profession recognize the reality under-
neath it.

It happens—irritatingly, more often than it should. Of course,
if the action is specified in the play, one's character would do it!
However unlikely a course of action it may seem to the youthful
actor, Hamlet kills Polonius in every performance. It is intrinsic to
Hamlet's character. The moment is nonnegotiable.

Yet, ridiculing such incidents is not my point. From an actor's
perspective, "My character wouldn't do that!" makes a weird kind
of sense. Actors frequently encounter challenging moments in
scripts. Characters often behave in ways contrary to common sense.
Almost everybody can see that Romeo's rash challenge to Tybalt is
ill-advised.

Acting asks us to enter the imaginative realm. For some of us,
that is all we need to know. When actors encounter the difficult
moment, they are frequently told, "Don't worry, it isn't real."

That response doesn't cut it with actors dedicated to finding organic truthfulness in their acting. To carry out the action noncommittally, or symbolically, is just as bad as not carrying it out at all. Either way, the audience is cheated. But there *is* a solution to this dilemma, a solution that asks us to recognize that there is more than one level of training.

Work on the Self

Up to now, we have been working on the acting instrument, the self. The previous chapters deal with learning to recognize the cognitive abilities underlying the acting process, fine-tuning them, and applying them. We have investigated layers of thought not normally open for inspection, because if we understand our organic thought processes, we can more faithfully reconstruct them when we act.

But this is only one part of an actor's work on the self. Learning to strengthen and properly use the voice, understanding the body and movement, reading widely in dramatic literature and the arts, and coming to appreciate the study of history all play an important part in an actor's development of her or his instrument.

Training both the mind and the body plays a central role in preparing to be an actor. But this is still not all. Once again, a comparison to athletes may be useful. Professional athletes need to prepare physically and mentally, but they also need to know how their game is played. Well-conditioned bodies and alert minds won't get athletes very far if they know nothing of the rules, the structure, or the timing of the contest in which they are participating.

The same is true of acting. Having explored and developed an interesting set of skills, it is time to turn our attention to how these are applied in the theatrical setting.

Work on the Role

Stanislavski's most widely recognized contribution to actor training was his delineation of how an actor's skills are applied to the creation of a role. The idea of separating work on the self from work on the role, like so much in contemporary actor training, was his.

Stanislavski believed that an actor's work could be subdivided into manageable steps: a play, and one's part in it, could be systematically studied and worked upon step by step. Once physically and mentally trained, actors still needed tools that would show them when and how to apply these skills to benefit the play and the ensemble.

Stanislavski experimented with a variety of approaches to accomplish this. The following process outlined is a distillation of ideas from many periods of his work, most closely hewing to his "method of physical actions," a formulation developed very late in his life.

> One word [Stanislavski] liked to use a lot was truth, which in this country has been usually interpreted to mean true to life, or else real, true emotions. In fact, Stanislavski could not have been more plain about what kind of truth he was talking about: "To play truly means to be right, logical, coherent, to think, strive, feel, and act in unison with your role."
> —Richard Hornby

Underlying all the steps that follow is the assumption that the actor comes with a sense of how to reach the creative state of mind on the sensory/perceptive level, on the social level, and on the verbal level. Those steps become second nature and are assumed to be engaged in any action that arises out of the analytical stages.

These analytical steps, the logical portion of the thought pyramid, have for too long been treated as if they were the first steps in acting. That is unfortunate, because logic is only a small part of our rich mental life. Engaging it too early, or to the exclusion of other realms of thought, creates a mechanical performance. Nevertheless, just because some have taken this portion of Stanislavski's work out of context, we cannot be blind to its importance. It is the culmination of his approach.

Putting Yourself in the Play

Stanislavski's most famous injunction, "Love the art in yourself, not yourself in the art," is the impetus for a set of steps to help the actor adjust mentally to participating in the play. It reminds us, "The play's the thing." First and foremost actors are to remember that their work is to serve the art form and the narrative, not to display their personal talent or success.

Starting from that premise, we first have to read the play wholistically, as literature. We need to think about the overall meaning of the play and the author's accomplishment. We may have to do some research to help us better understand and appreciate it.

Figure 11.1. You become the character by adopting the character's perspective.

Of particular importance is excavating all the clues to the given circumstances. (This is explored thoroughly in Chapter 5.) We must discover *and sensorially create* our character's situation. We need to comb the text carefully for references to situation. Clues may also come from stage directions, references in the dialogue, costumes, scenery, and properties. These may be specified in great detail in the script, but more often they are simply implied and must be amplified with historical research. These details may also be altered by the director (for example, she may choose to set the play in some other period than the one specified in the text), in which case the director's decisions take precedence.

Assuming the Character's Perspective

The second stage of the analytical process is to begin thinking of yourself in the character's situation, in the first person. One assumes the character by seeing the play through the character's eyes.

This is the step where innocent beginners go wrong, and find themselves declaring what their characters would and wouldn't do. We do not accomplish this step by thinking of ourselves as the character. If we believe we *are* Hamlet, we are not acting; we are insane.

If we think of our present-day selves in the character's place, like the Yankee in King Arthur's court, we find ourselves making irrational substitutions (responding to Hamlet's predicament by saying, "I think I'd just shoot Claudius," for example).

Instead we think, *If* I were in this situation, what might lead me to undertake these actions? Stanislavski called this the "magic if," and properly used, it is transformative. In this formulation neither the situation nor the actions are negotiable. This is an exercise in adopting the character's viewpoint, not replacing it with our own. Seeing the world of the play through the character's eyes means adopting the character's worldview and the assumptions that arise through his or her experience, as well as the immediate lines and actions.

Finding the Units

The third stage of the analytical process is to subdivide scenes in the play into smaller units for the purpose of closer scrutiny. It's like the silly children's riddle: How do you eat an elephant? One bite at a time.

Thinking about plays in terms that are too general can lead actors to miss important nuances of their parts. Stanislavski urged his casts to split the play into units of playable action. These units have traditionally been called *beats* in the American theatre, because that is what the first Russian émigrés called them in their New York studios. The term, so evocative of musical associations, came into widespread use before anyone realized that the teachers were saying *bits* with thick accents. So *beats* they still are.

A typical beat runs from a half-page to a full page, though the length can vary greatly. A beat encompasses one subject or one line of action, as a paragraph does in prose. Too many short beats subvert a sense of momentum and continuation. Too few, and there are long, mind-numbing stretches. A new beat often begins when a character enters or exits, when a character dramatically changes the subject, or when a line of action is complete.

The important thing to remember about dividing a script into beats is that the process is meant to help. There isn't one, and only one, right way to do it. It is a tool for examining the script more closely, an aid in the analytical process. And beats can always be changed later if further study leads to a new view of the script.

The next four steps are at the heart of Stanislavski's system of text analysis. They are the tools by which to steer a performance so that it stays in line with the intentions of the playwright and the needs of the ensemble. Unfortunately, there is no commonly accepted terminology for these four steps, in part because Stanislavski gave different names to them in different stages of his work, and more especially because the many translators publishing in English have not always agreed on the best equivalent words.

Specifying What Is Happening

For each beat, you want to note what the character is doing (as specified by the script). Some of the more frequently used terms here are *activity* and *task*. For your purpose, you want to write down exactly what the script says you are doing. Examples might be *talking with a friend* or *waiting for a train.*

Defining the Objective

Stanislavski observed that we undertake actions, consciously or unconsciously, to accomplish goals in life. Likewise, on the stage, we don't just do things because the script says to do them. That would be the mindless repetition that we have been studying to avoid. It is important that

> *Being aware of your intention from instant to instant is one of the most important facets of your work. It will give you purpose, and it will give the scene an emotional thrust. Most of your energy will be a consequence of how strongly you play the intent and how important it is to you that the intent be fulfilled.*
> —Tony Barr

you (as an actor) understand why your character is doing whatever she or he is doing, even if your character may not be so clear on the reason. (Characters, like people, sometimes take refuge in lack of clarity, or even lie to themselves, but you as an actor must see beyond that to fully portray them.)

Specifying what your character hopes to accomplish is the step that will allow you to *choose* your actions. This book adopts a common term for this analytical step, defining the *objective*, but it is also frequently called the *motivation*, the *victory*, or the *goal*. Again, the term is less important than the step. Michael Shurtleff, a well-known author on acting and auditioning, says that what you want to write down is the answer to the question, What are you fighting for? This sensible suggestion avoids a name altogether, but helps you focus on your character's desires.

Write your answer in a very specific form, which will help you use it to get you into the action. Start your answer with the words

I want to and follow them immediately with an active verb. It is therefore a statement of something you want to do. Be very careful not to write down something passive. *I want to be rich* isn't an objective, it is a wish. *I want to earn a million dollars* is better. It needs to be something that can be acted.

While you're at it, you ought to write in a form that engages your imagination. The objective for the activity *waiting for a train* might be something like *I want to escape this dreary small-town existence,* but you might respond more directly to something colloquial, like *I want to blow this pop stand.* You will not be sharing these statements with anyone, so write whatever captures for you a sense of what you (as a character) hope to accomplish.

Don't write in a negative form, or use a negative in the sentence. *I don't want to get caught* is better rendered as *I want to escape. I just want everybody to leave me alone* comes out better as *I want to get away from all these people.*

Be exact and detailed about one beat at a time. Each objective is for one beat, not for the character's whole life. *I want to find happiness* is much too general when *I want to persuade James to go on a date with me* is the goal you have in mind. If you are not sure if your objective is specific enough, ask yourself, How will I know if I have accomplished this? In the latter case James will say yes. In the former, it is hard to know if you have found happiness. It needs more specificity.

Defining the objective will help you decide what you will choose to do in rehearsal, but it is mostly meant to help you keep your actions in line with the play. It is imperative that these statements of the character's goals derive from a careful reading of the script. At this point, you are trying to align your personal skills as an actor with the requirements of the play. Your objective, therefore, is not a statement of what you, personally, want in your life. It is not even a statement of what you, personally, want for your character. It is your best thinking on what the character's intentions (as created by the playwright) are.

You should have only one objective for every beat, and it should be the main point of the beat, not a small subdesire. In fact, the most typical way to define beats is that one starts every time your character has a new objective and it ends when the goal is accomplished (you get on the train and leave) or is decidedly frustrated (you discover that the train no longer stops at this station). At that point a new objective begins, and the cycle repeats.

Characters don't always get their desires. Hamlet dies before he can become king, but his goals include trying with all his might to gain the throne. Don't let your knowledge of the outcome outweigh your intuition about what you (as the character) want. Fight with all your might for what you want, even if the play denies it in the end.

You will probably notice that cleverly constructed plays often put characters with opposite desires on stage together. Conflicts arise from the fact that the thing you want, and are trying hard to get, is precisely what somebody else doesn't want you to have and is trying to prevent you from getting. If this is the case, then you probably have a good objective! (Who wants to see a play about a character that hopes to get rich, instantly wins the lottery, and quickly exits on her way to Paris? Great for her, boring for us.)

Pursuing the Objective

Once you know what you want, your task has just begun. The real question is how you will go about getting it. For each beat, after you have specified your activity and your objective, brainstorm ways (within the circumstances of the play) that you, as the character, might go about achieving your goals. While there is only one objective per beat, several possible ways to get what you want may be appropriate.

You may charm another character to get her to agree with you, but you could also threaten or emotionally blackmail or pout. From your brainstormed list you want to eliminate any ideas that are incompatible with the information in the play, but you may be surprised at the wide range of possibilities open to you.

These ideas, often called *tactics* or *actions,* are not detailed, predetermined plans for exactly what you will do. Rather, they are thoughts about ways you could try. In rehearsal these are the avenues you will use to *change another character.* Approach them precisely as you approached the change-your-partner's-behavior exercise. If you decide that you will put your fingers in your mouth, pull it into a stupid face, and then make exactly two unusual noises in order to get someone to smile, you are apt to fail. These plans are too restrictive and don't take into account the other person's responses. A more general plan to amuse him or charm him will allow you more room to improvise on the spot until you succeed.

You want to leave yourself room to see what works, both for you and for the other actor(s). It may be that an idea sounds great in theory but has little effect in practice. You need a backup plan, and a backup for your backup, at the very least. A dozen or so ideas from which to experiment is not out of line.

Investing in the Action

The final stage of beat work is to seek a personal investment in the process. Stanislavski's comments on this subject are few and vague, but he experimented throughout his career with techniques to help actors find a personal connection with their work. His pupil Vakhtangov named this process *justification*. Many use the term *substitution*.

This is where the actor first creates an empathetic connection to his character. The actor playing Hamlet, for example, must fulfill the play's given circumstance that his father has been murdered. With sufficient imagination, perhaps, an actor can explore what this might feel like to him, but the likelihood that one's father has actually been murdered is small and certainly not a prerequisite to play the part.

It is not uncommon to find, as a first reaction, that this is not an immediately evocative circumstance. It doesn't always create an instant connection—that I-know-how-that-feels identification.

If it does, great; if not, actors may want to explore their own experience to find something *similar to* what's going on in the play. The actor may think, *I've never been cheated out of a kingship, but it's like the time I unfairly lost a role to the producer's son.* It is even possible to identify with a fiction: *I've never lost a kingship, but I'd probably feel as if I had been cheated out of my inheritance. I've never had that happen to me either, but I can more easily imagine what it would be like and how I would feel.*

Putting It Together

Having taken the play apart, the last stage of analysis is putting it together again. You do this by looking at a master list of all your objectives and seeing what unites them. From this you distill one *superobjective* for the whole play. This is a statement of goal that will help align your performance with the playwright's overarching theme. This statement is not necessarily the same as any individual objective you have, but it will be compatible with all of them. It is a statement of the broadest kind. The character who was earlier leaving town by train might be seeking a superobjective like *I want to seek a new freedom in my life.*

The superobjective is a guiding vision of what the play, and the character's part in it, is about. It isn't intimately associated with the moment-to-moment choices you will make as an actor, but is an overview of your big desires. It helps you reflect on the nature of the role as a whole.

> **performance exercise**
>
> **analyzing a scene**

This exercise is best done as homework, at your own pace. You'll need the script of a scene on which you are working.

1. Divide this scene into beats. Take a colored pencil and draw a line across the page at each beat change. Number beats consecutively. Some actors find it helpful to give beats individual names, or short headlinelike descriptors ("Romeo Gets Married" or "Lady Macbeth Takes Charge!").
2. For each numbered beat, in the margins or on a blank facing page, write a short phrase describing the physical activity taking place.
3. Under that description, using the I-want-to-do format, write your objective for this beat.
4. Under your objective, write a half dozen or so ideas about how you might achieve this objective.
5. Under these ideas, write an as-if statement for any objectives with which you desire a closer connection.
6. At the end of the scene, write the superobjective that encompasses your vision of it as a whole.

Student Portraits

Although the group has been working well together for some time, anxiety levels are high about this more traditional school-type work. The students are not used to seeing one another in this guise, and the written work has changed the dynamic. Some of the stronger personalities are newly subdued, while a few shy types are suddenly outgoing.

The instructor asks everyone in the group to trade scripts with another class member to compare notes. Though everyone is working on different scenes, a second set of eyes can help clarify things.

There is wide variation in the number of beats. Some students have found several to a page; Susan has found only one division in a ten-page scene. Talking with his partner helps James see that his division of every line into a separate beat is excessive. The paragraph metaphor helps: paragraphs tend not to be one sentence long. James decides that several of his initial beats can be grouped together. Once he has done so, he realizes the same principle applies throughout. He decides to work a bit more conservatively.

Susan, who had found only one division, soon sees that her beats are too long to manage efficiently. They cover too much territory. She has listed several physical actions for each beat; they are brief and straightforward, but the instructor reminds her that each beat should have only one action.

The instructor says that they need to spend a good deal of time looking at objectives. He first checks to see whether the objectives all begin with the words *I want*. Most do, but a few begin *I will* or *I need*. These need to be rewritten, and the class does so as a group. One objective has the forbidden negative in it, and that too is immediately reworded.

Checking for active verbs takes more time. Many students' first attempts contain passive constructions. First, all the *I want to be* sentences, and there are several, are changed to indicate an action. "I want to get famous," causes a little debate, but grammatically it just means, *I want to be famous. Get* can be active, when it means retrieving, but here it is still passive. It takes a while before everyone sees that many verbs besides *to be* can be passive.

The instructor is about to move on when Amy raises a question about "I want power." This objective avoids the passive construction, but it is not an action. The instructor first says the statement has no verb, but the student who listed this objective declares that *want* is so a verb. It is in fact the formula the instructor has asked them to use. The instructor is forced to concede, but reminds the class that *I want* is only part of the formula, which in its entirety is *I want to do something. I want* is a wish, not an action.

Since objectives are not easy to write, the instructor suggests they work on "I want power" for a moment. Everyone in the group tries to improve it, one person at a time:

I want power.

I want to get power.

I want to gain power.

I want to win power.

I want to have power over my enemies.

I want to win power to use over my enemies.

I want to crush my competitors.

I want to destroy my competitors.

I want to challenge [another character], who has power over me.

I want to challenge and defeat [the character with the power].

The switch from "I want to win power" to "I want to have power" is fiercely contested, but the instructor allows each student to work on the statement as he or she sees fit. Step-by-step improvement is the goal. Afterward, the class agrees that the statement has gotten better as it has gotten more active, as it has become more specifically aimed at one target instead of all the play's antagonists, and as it has delineated something the achievement of which can be clearly determined.

The instructor now urges the group not to be satisfied with their first attempts. "Go back and see if you can improve your objectives," he suggests.

At first this becomes something of a thesaurus game, everyone suggesting alternative wordings, but the class gets noticeably better at making their objectives more active, more specific, and more assessable.

Eventually the group moves on to looking at tactical statements. Most of the students have been able to see only one or two approaches, but a little brainstorming usually turns up a half dozen to a dozen more. Some suggestions are wildly out of keeping with the play, because students aren't always familiar with their classmates' play choices, but four or five good new possibilities is a typical yield.

The instructor urges the students to work the same way when they're by themselves: brainstorm wildly, then edit down to good possibilities. Editing as you go leads to a censorious frame of mind and too little creativity.

The instructor is reluctant to look too closely at students' as-if choices, since these can be rather personal. But a couple of students volunteer a statement or two for group examination because they're not sure whether they're approaching this part of the exercise correctly.

Susan is working on a play about a woman who cares for her aged, and now senile, mother. Her as-if statement at first seems identical to the situation in the play: "It is as if my mother had a stroke." She points out, though, that she can't imagine her own mother being senile, because her mother is still quite young. The stroke is a substitution that seems more plausible to her, and brings the play closer to home. The instructor agrees. Susan's statement is a good example of why we use as-if statements.

Sam, who is working on a play about the assassination of President Kennedy, which occurred before Sam was born, volunteers that he found John Lennon's death comparable. His classmates protest, arguing that the political weight of the two events is not equal. As they talk, however, it becomes clearer that finding an exact parallel is not the point. Lennon's murder holds the emotional weight that helps Sam imagine what a character hearing of Kennedy's death may have felt. He is using what he knows to understand the play better. The instructor again confirms that this is good use of the technique.

"What do we do with this stuff?" asks Marcus when the session is over.

"That," says the instructor, "is an excellent question. We'll talk about that next time."

An Example of Analyzing a Scene

The following scene is an excerpt from *The Seagull*, the play that brought Stanislavski's Moscow Art Theatre to world attention. The seagull became the logo of the theatre, Chekhov became recognized around the world, and Stanislavski added the role of Trigorin to his list of brilliant successes.

The scene takes place halfway through the second act. Earlier the character Konstantin had written an amateur play, which was performed by Nina, a young aspiring actress with whom he is in love. The play was not well received. Nina is dazzled with an older author, Trigorin, and her indifference makes Konstantin frantic.

Dividing the Scene into Beats

Beat #1 ─────────────────────────────────

(Nina is sitting alone in a park near a lake. Konstantin Treplev enters without a hat, carrying a gun and a dead seagull)
KONSTANTIN: Are you alone?
    NINA: Yes, I am.
(Konstantin lays the seagull at her feet)

Beat #2 ─────────────────────────────────

    NINA: What does that mean?
KONSTANTIN: I was cruel enough to kill this seagull today. I lay it at your feet.
    NINA: What's the matter with you? *(She picks up the seagull and looks at it)*
KONSTANTIN: *(After a pause)* Soon I'll kill myself in the same way.
    NINA: I hardly know you anymore.

Beat #3 ─────────────────────────────────

KONSTANTIN: I hardly know you either. You've changed toward me. Your eyes are cold. You are embarrassed to be near me.
    NINA: You've become so irritable lately. Whenever you say anything, I can't understand you. You talk in symbols. And this seagull, I suppose, is another symbol. Excuse me, but I don't understand . . . *(Puts the seagull down on a bench)* I'm too simple to understand.
KONSTANTIN: This began the night my play failed. Women never forgive failure. I've burnt the whole play, every last page. If you only knew how unhappy I am. Your indifference is horrible . . . It's like I woke up and found this lake suddenly dried up or vanished into the earth. You say you are too simple to understand me. What is there to understand? My play failed, which you never liked anyway, and now you think of me as mediocre and worthless, like everybody else does. *(Stamping his foot)* I understand perfectly, it's like a nail being driven into my head. To hell with it, and to hell with my pride. It's sucking my blood like a leech.

Beat #4 —————————————————————————————

> *(Sees Trigorin, who enters reading a book)* Here comes the real genius, like Hamlet with his book. *(Mocking)* "Words, words, words. . . ." This sun has barely reached you, but already you're smiling. You are melting in his rays. I won't stand in your way. *(Exits quickly leaving Nina bewildered)*

Analyzing the Scene Beat by Beat

The possible division of the scene marked is from the perspective of the actor playing Konstantin. The first two beats are somewhat shorter than is common in most plays, but in each case the conversation shifts quickly to a new topic so a new beat is called for.

Beat #1

Physical action: Finding Nina and laying the seagull at her feet.
Objective: I want to get Nina's attention.
Tactics: Shock, stare, insult, surprise, act irrationally.
As if: It is as if I am trying to impress the popular girl in my high school class, even though she will not give me the time of day.

The physical description above is straightforward and brief. It is relatively objective, and everyone can probably agree on it.

The objective listed is just one possibility. It is a statement (in the first person) that specifies what Konstantin wants. It is assessable, in that it is possible to tell whether he has Nina's attention or not. It is capable of being acted. Several possible ways of going about it are listed under tactics.

The as-if is very subjective. It is not a statement about the play but a rough equivalent that might stimulate the imagination to intuit the emotional weight of the scene and the nature of the relationship. It might also suggest some more tactic possibilities. As the actor, I would not play this directly in rehearsal. It is a jumping off point to get me involved in the scene. Ideally, it will not be necessary because the scene and my partner will be stimulating enough. It is a tool, there if I need it.

This beat changes very quickly because the goal is achieved. I want Nina's undivided attention, which the lines indicate she gives me. As the actor, I would not play this directly in rehearsal. The action of laying the dead bird at her feet absolutely confirms that she will attend to me for a brief time, at least. Therefore, I need a new objective.

Beat #2

Physical action: Making an announcement.
Objective: I want to impress Nina with the gravity of the situation.
Tactics: Threaten, stun, pronounce, break down.
As if: It is as if my parents have forbidden me to go to a party, so I throw a door-slamming tantrum to try to get my way.

This beat is also somewhat short, because the thing I want (as Konstantin) seems to be denied me. I threaten suicide, but Nina brushes it off as a juvenile tantrum. Her response ends this section and pushes us on to another beat. Notice that the reason—the objective is no longer achievable—is the opposite of why the first beat ended—that objective was accomplished. This process, however, is the same either way. You try as hard as you can to get your objective until you succeed or conclusively fail.

Beat #3

Physical action: Confronting Nina.
Objective: I want to win back Nina's love.
Tactics: Beg, ridicule, reason, amuse, humiliate, explain, taunt, demand, plead.
As if: It is as if I have been denied a raise on my job, and I argue with my boss to get the decision reversed.

This beat is the center of the scene. Though it contains the fewest overt actions of any of the four beats (just stamping the foot), it has the fullest plot and emotional content of them all. As Konstantin, my actions are the most crucial. I desperately want to get Nina's love back. As an actor, I cannot help but notice that Konstantin may not be going about this very well. Many of his statements are ill advised. My job is not to judge him, however, but to find a way to put myself in his shoes. To be honest, at his age I didn't always handle my romantic affairs very well either, so I can empathize.

The as-if for this scene is not romantic at all. It seems unrelated to the play. Remember that its purpose is not to restate the play exactly, but to give me something to help remind myself of the importance of the scene. I can imagine being unfairly denied a raise, and I can guess that I might be so upset over it that I would not handle the confrontation well. This as-if may not work for you. These are personal, and very subjective, statements. Perhaps thinking about talking your way out of a traffic ticket would be closer to home for you. Try to find something that creates in you an empathy for the character's actions to get you started thinking about the scene.

The more common statement, of course, would be something like *It is as if a girl rejected me, and I want to win her back.* That is little more than an exact restatement of the plot, but if you can feel the import of this circumstance directly, then that is all that is needed. The previous as-if statement is to assist in reaching an empathetic response if one does not automatically follow from the text.

Beat #4

Physical action: Mocking a rival.
Objective: I want to expose Trigorin's pretension.
Tactics: Mimic, disdain, pout, brood, sneer, ignore, sulk, ridicule.
As if: It is as if the neighborhood bully comes to the park, and I mimic him from a safe distance.

The final beat begins with the entrance of Trigorin. A new character coming onstage is almost always occasion for a new beat. The beat is brief because Konstantin chooses to exit rather than stay and confront Trigorin directly.

Superobjective

Looking at the four beats as a whole I can see that they are all concerned with my relationship to Nina. I might state the overall objective of the scene as something like this: I want to win Nina's love.

If I were to analyze the whole play I might also notice that I have other very similar scenes with Nina and with my mother as well. I might state my goal for the play as follows: I want to win the love and respect I deserve.

This is, of course, not the only way (or even the best way) to play Konstantin. There are many possible approaches, but by committing myself to these choices I have a way of steering the performance, night after night, in ways that are in line with the narrative of the play. That is the primary purpose of an objective.

Journal Entry: Objectives

Because the work associated with this chapter is largely written, you needn't redo it in your journal. See if you can put copies of all your work with the journal so you can consult it in the future. Don't let it get lost.

It may be helpful to write out all the steps in improving one objective so you can see the way you work through the stages of examining and refining. Take a journal page and write down each successive entry.

Related Optional Exercises

1. Look over your script to find every piece of information that is news to your character at the moment he or she hears it. These are "discoveries." Try to imagine what it is like not to know this information. What does your character feel as a result of learning this new piece of information? Try to break out of routine. Look for everything that is new to your character. (Of course, you have read the play before so it is not new to you, the actor. Part of putting yourself in your character's shoes, however, is imagining his or her ignorance.)

2. Do something routine, such as pacing off the size of a room. Now see how much stronger and more interesting you can make the activity by finding an important reason for doing it. For example, pace it off because you have inherited some valuable antique furniture, which may be too large for this space. See if it will fit. Or imagine that you are about to trade apartments with another person and you want to be sure that you are not being cheated in the deal. Notice that the reason for the action (the goal, the objective) is much more important than the action itself. The intensity of your commitment comes from your reason for undertaking the action, not from the action.

3. Get together with a group of friends and conduct a group analysis of a scene from a famous play. Individually write a superobjective for each of the characters in the scene, then

do a detailed analysis of one character. As a group, compare
notes and see whether you can improve your analysis. Did
anybody notice details that you missed? Are there any wordings of objectives that you find more exciting than those
you chose?

12 A Scene in Performance

I feel like I know a lot of things *about* acting now," Michael is saying, "but not how to act." His is an intelligent comment, accurately reflecting his situation. Like Michael, you have been collecting the skills you need to act but have not yet assembled them into a complete package. It is like buying all the ingredients for a cake and realizing you don't know how to bake.

Fortunately, once you have all the skills assembled, acting is as simple as baking a cake. You mix things together, put them in the right environment, and the combination of ingredients transforms itself.

culminating exercise

performing a scene

With a partner, select and prepare a five-minute scene from a realistic play written in the last decade. The scene does not have to be as fully produced as it would be for public performance, but there should be a suggestion of the set and costumes. A table may stand in for a bar, or a row of chairs for a couch, but don't leave anything you need unrepresented. Incorporate actual objects for all the props used in the scene. (Don't mime a letter or a telephone, for example.)

The following instructions are very detailed, telling you what to do every step of the way. Don't let their length daunt you. Nothing new is being thrown into the mix. This is just a suggested protocol for combining the skills you are already familiar with into a performance.

There are many other good ways to do this. These instructions are not the only way; they are *a* way. As you become more confident, you may want to modify them. This sequence is a blueprint to get you started until you have enough experience to determine what does and doesn't work for you.

There are two stages in mounting a scene: rehearsal and performance. These stages are fundamentally different from each other in the way they are carried out.

Rehearsal

What follows is a step-by-step guide to rehearsing a scene—a map of when and how to apply the skills that you have learned in the previous chapters.

Step 1: Meet with your partner to plan the process

When rehearsing a scene with another person, you need to make a time commitment, develop a trusting relationship, and be disciplined and dependable. When something goes wrong in a scene, it is almost always traceable to flawed preparation, usually a failure of rehearsal discipline.

At your first meeting, make arrangements about how to get in touch with each other: trade telephone numbers (including cell and work numbers), fax numbers, and/or e-mail addresses so that you will be able to contact each other when you need to.

You should also schedule rehearsal times and places. Fitting your rehearsals into existing schedules may be quite difficult. We all lead busy lives. It is usually easier to schedule all your rehearsals at the first meeting rather than plan them one at a time. A regular schedule at a regular place (every Tuesday and Friday evening at 7:00 P.M. at the community center) is easier to recall and honor than a random arrangement.

A good rule of thumb is to schedule at least an hour of rehearsal time with your partner and an hour of personal time to work on the scene alone for every minute of performance time. A five-minute scene, then, needs five hours of joint rehearsal and five hours of individual attention. Hour-long rehearsals seem to work best. A day or two between rehearsals is helpful, but more than four days between rehearsals is usually too long.

Ideally, you'll want to meet twice a week for three weeks. Each rehearsal should be long enough for you to arrive, arrange your workspace, warm up a bit, and then work for one full hour. If you like to socialize, leave yourself additional time for a bit of conversation before and after the work session.

Either agree to use the remaining steps outlined here as a plan of attack, or specifically discuss any alterations to it. Be sure you both commit to the plan, and then alter it only in an emergency. Plain old dependability will go a long way toward creating the trust relationship you want and need. Be on time and ready to work for all meetings and rehearsals. (This may seem a minor point, but in a collaborative art like theatre, where nothing can begin until everyone is present, waiting even a couple of minutes becomes a real irritation.) Being late is bad theatrical etiquette. Being present but so preoccupied with other business that rehearsal cannot begin is worse!

If you don't know your partner well, take a few minutes to become acquainted at this first meeting. It is not necessary for you to become friends to work well together, but it will help with scene selection if you know something about your partner's interests and personality. Agree to bring some scene possibilities to your next meeting.

In between Step 1 and Step 2
Look at material that may be suitable for you and your partner. Don't panic if you are not well read in drama—few beginners are—but spend some time looking at plays with scenes for two people who fit you and your partner's general profiles. Some suggestions for material appear at the end of this book in the Resources section. For a first scene, contemporary realism is preferable to verse plays or those involving theatrical styles with which you are unfamiliar. There are books full of sample scenes in the performing arts section of your local bookstore or available online. These are generally inexpensive, so it might be to your benefit to pick one up and read through it.

Scenes used as exercises should usually be about five minutes long. They are best when they contain action rather than just narration. Select several possibilities that interest you, that are exciting. Don't make the mistake of choosing a bland scene because you're frightened about performing more challenging material. Go for strong characters; they are more rewarding to play in the long run.

Comedy is difficult to perform and often depends on advanced acting skills like good timing, physical dexterity, and verbal inflection. Be cautious about committing to purely comedic choices. (See the section on comedy at the end of the book for more information about this point.)

Eliminate from your list any scenes that you are not willing to perform as written. It is perfectly acceptable to bypass characters whose actions or words offend you, but it is not ethical to rewrite an author's material to come closer to your personal taste.

Look at your list of possibilities to see that the scenes are well balanced, with roughly the same amount of dialogue for the two characters, and that the characters are suited to you and your partner. Characters who are much older or younger than the person who will play them often present more problems than rewards. For this exercise it is *not* necessary, however, that you be bound by gender and/or racial assumptions made in the text. (Doctors, for example, are often identified as Caucasian males, but there is nothing in the script that would preclude an African American female from playing most of them.) Be open to the possibilities.

Step 2: Choose the scene

Bring copies of all the scenes you have on your list of possibilities to the second meeting with your partner. Plan to arrive at this meeting a few minutes early. It will help demonstrate your dependability, and it will give you a moment to collect your thoughts.

With your partner, look at all the scenes the two of you have brought. Pay special attention to any play that both of you selected, even if you each brought a different scene from it. It will probably take you the full hour of this rehearsal to read the best possibilities aloud and discuss the pros and cons of your short list. Don't agree to perform anything that you deeply dislike, but be as open as possible to your partner's interests and suggestions. At this session you are not only selecting a scene, you are learning how to work together.

Learn what you can about your partner as a person from how she reveals herself in the selection process.

If you both have brought several choices in, there ought to be something you can both agree on by the end of the hour. If you cannot find mutually acceptable material, establish specific criteria for a further search and schedule an *extra* selection session.

When you do find a piece with which you are both happy, be sure you each have a copy of the scene, and decide specifically where the scene will begin and end. (Editing out minor characters who interrupt for a line or two is common practice.) If you don't each have a copy of the entire play, arrange to exchange it so that both of you can read the complete script before the next rehearsal.

In between Step 2 and Step 3

Read—twice—the complete play from which your scene is taken. Read it the first time as literature, with no agenda except enjoying it. The second time, read it with great care for clues to the given circumstances. Though you will only be performing one scene from the play, important clues about your character and the world of the play will be scattered throughout the text. It will help your future work if you make notes of your discoveries.

Silently improvise some of the activities of the play. Do a sensory exploration of an object (perhaps a prop specified by the text) to help you find the creative state of mind. Look again at the instructions for the exercise in Chapter 4 for a reminder about how to do this. Once you have felt the shift to this other way of thinking, practice doing some of the commonplace actions of your character using the everyday-task exercise in Chapter 5.

Spend a little time imagining where your specific scene might take place. If it is a room, decide how it might be arranged (in the real world, not on a stage). If it is an outdoor location or some large public place, think of real places you know that are similar.

Step 3: The first rehearsal

Arrive for this rehearsal in plenty of time to organize yourself and to arrange the things you need to improvise a space. Bring any small props (a telephone, for example) with you. Visit the restroom, finish your soft drink, and be ready to work when your partner arrives at the appointed time.

Begin the rehearsal with a brief warm-up. You may have a

warm-up ritual, but if not, see if your partner is willing to share one. (You can also look at the brief section on relaxation in this book for some possibilities.) This should occupy the first five or ten minutes of the rehearsal.

For the second ten minutes, do a see-and-be-seen exercise with your partner. This will help you learn more about your partner, deepen the trust between you, and (if you treat your partner's face like a sensory object) help you access the creative state of mind. (If your partner doesn't want to do the exercise, you can always do a sensory exploration of an object to get into the creative state.)

For the next fifteen minutes or so, pull two chairs up facing each other, sit so that your and your partner's knees are almost touching, and explore the scene. Because all the traps that faced you when you first added speech to your acting are still there, interact with your partner in an entirely different way than just reading to each other.

Look at your text and, on the spot, memorize your first line of dialogue. This will only take a second. You are not trying for long-term recall; you just want to learn it well enough to look up from your text. Look right into your partner's eyes and say (not read) the line to him. Ask your partner to interrupt you and make you do the line again if you start speaking before you look at him, or if you look away before finishing.

If you have a second sentence to this speech, look down at the text again, memorize this line, and look into your partner's eyes to say this line. Continue in this fashion until you get to the end of your first speech. Have your partner use the same procedure to deliver his lines back to you.

Do this twice, with no discussion. Just go through the scene. On the third read-through, switch parts. This will help you see the scene as a whole. You'll learn more about the other character in the scene, and you will hear from your partner something about how he views and understands your character.

You are now over halfway through the first rehearsal. You will probably begin to learn a lot about the scene from this exercise. Let your work encompass your new understanding, but at this stage don't make a specific effort to "act."

It is best not to interrupt your work with much small talk or discussion. You and your partner are trying to learn about the scene through your actions rather than through negotiated agreements.

Figure 12.1. You can mock up the furniture for a scene out of materials on hand. Three chairs become a couch for this improvising actor.

Trust that your partner is sensitive (literally, as in using sensory skills) to your ideas.

Now is a good time to introduce you to an important rule of theatrical courtesy: Never direct your partner, nor allow your partner to direct you. The term *partner* means you are equal collaborators. If you feel something is necessary for the scene to proceed, ask for it, but remember that your partner is not obligated to provide what you want. (From the character's point of view, your partner is often frustrating your objectives on purpose, having objectives that are the opposite of yours.) If your partner breaks the rule and tells you what to do, use the standard theatrical dodge, "Let's just see what develops in the next run-through."

For the final part of your rehearsal, try out some arrangements of the playing space. This will require some discussion, but keep it to a minimum. At this point you are not concerned with a final space arrangement but with a logical and intelligent interpretation of the script. With available materials, improvise an arrangement of your room or location that would be plausible for the action if it were really occurring.

Perhaps you and your partner may want to hold this first rehearsal in a real place similar to that described in your scene. A field trip to the park might be very useful if that is where your scene takes place. Visit a real museum or coffee shop to soak up some details to use in creating the given circumstances. In these cases, you probably won't be able to rearrange anything; just select an area in which to work.

Using either of these methods, you and your partner need to agree about the specifics of where you are. These are, of course, the given circumstances. As always, don't be only intellectual about things. Try to arrange the space and *feel* it.

For the final part of this rehearsal, using the environment that you and your partner have created or found, walk through the required actions of the scene without using the words in the script. Instead, say something like, *First I do this. Next I do that.* You will have to consult your script, but don't say the lines. Just work on specifying and choosing the steps in the physical activity in the scene. (This should feel very much like the sixteen-steps exercise in Chapter 10.) Your purpose is to become physically comfortable with the activity of the scene and to learn about the scene from the bottom of the thought pyramid up. You are doing the first work of the scene in the sensorial realm. If you have time, run the scene again, saying no before you say yes.

> *When I'm in the rehearsal room, and I'm doing run-throughs, I get to the point where I really feel like I can start acting. I've developed a relationship with the other character, I pretty much know what I'm doing all the way through, I've made decisions about the character's body, and I know the parameters within which the other actors and I are responding. I'm free and I can play.*
> —Stephen Spinella

Throughout this session, keep your attention primarily on the sensory level. The goal is to find and maintain the creative state of mind. Though you have done some interacting with a partner and have used the words of the script, today's rehearsal is designed to allow you to build a sensorial foundation to your scene.

In between Step 3 and Step 4

Sit with your script and analyze it as outlined in Chapter 11. Begin by dividing your scene into beats. Then, for each beat, determine your objective, brainstorm some tactics for achieving it, and, if you want to personalize the scene, specify an as-if.

Step 4: The second look at the scene

In this second rehearsal, you and your partner will be mainly working on adding the social layer of the thought pyramid to the firm sensory foundation you created during the previous rehearsal. You will be doing many different kinds of things, but try to keep your attention on the interaction with your partner.

Once again, it is a good idea for you and your partner to begin with a warm-up and a see-and-be-seen exercise. To get to the social layer today you may want to begin to think about your partner's personality. If your partner were to undertake the actions of her character in real life, how would she go about it? How would she express the emotions of the character? You may want to think about the extremes of your partner's character's behavior and begin to imagine your partner with those abilities and qualities.

The process of imagining your partner as the character is often called *endowment*. It is a kind of fantasizing about your partner, which is a normal part of acting. As a point of etiquette, however, actors do not share these fantasies with each other. They belong only to the stage, and should not bleed over into life offstage. Like other kinds of fantasies, they lose much of their magic when said aloud. Imagine away, and let the power of your imagination endow your partner's performance, but keep your thoughts to yourself.

You will be about fifteen minutes into rehearsal at this point. Quickly organize the performance space into the arrangement you and your partner agreed on at the last meeting. If you need to take a second to regain the creative state of mind, do so through a short sensory exploration.

With your script in one hand, walk through the activities of the scene. Today you will also add speech, so as you did during the seated rehearsal a few days ago, try to learn a line at a time and look up from the script to deliver it instead of just reading it.

You not only need to make choices about your actions, you need to make strong ones. Your actions must affect your partner. The only exceptions are fight scenes and love scenes, which have the potential for violence or sexual harassment. In these cases, the actors and the director (if there is one) must know what is going to happen in advance. These scenes must be carefully planned with the consent of all involved. You don't need to avoid such scenes. It is hard to name a great play that doesn't contain them. They are some of the most exciting and challenging scenes in all of literature. But they must be properly prepared. Because these need to be carefully choreographed and discussed, you'll deal with them at a later rehearsal. If your scene contains such a situation, just try saying, "This is where we fight [or kiss]." For now, pick the scene up at the first available point after the activity.

This is a bit complicated. You will be trying to read lines, carry out the activities of the scene, and make choices all at once. It is normal if you lose your place in the script from time to time. This time through, the scene is apt to be slow and laborious. Don't let that worry you. Don't cut corners. Incorporate the lines, the actions, and the choices into the process, however slow it may be.

It helps if you let the script in your hand become a scene prop, like a fan or a plate, whenever possible. Use it, instead of letting it be an additional concern. Point with it. Wave with it. Let it help you during the moments you are not consulting it.

Work through the scene in this fashion once or twice. It may begin to develop a life of its own. If the story or the relationship begins to emerge in stronger form of its own accord, allow it but don't force it. There is no hurry. You are just exploring the scene.

By the third run-through or so, you are ready to develop the exchange between you and your partner further. Consult your notes briefly, and get your objective clearly in mind. If it is inspiring you—stirring up your acting juices—then you are ready to proceed. If it is not connecting strongly, consult your as-if statements to help you focus on the personal impact of your objective.

By the way, objectives and as-ifs, like many parts of the actor's craft, are traditionally not shared. It is not important that your partner know what you have chosen for an objective nor how you have personalized it. In fact, the more a partner knows from nontheatrical exchange, the harder it will be to react honestly to your onstage actions. If he knows too specifically what you are trying or thinking, he will be looking ahead and reacting to the idea instead of the reality. Let your partner be surprised.

You are about to begin a run-through of the scene during which you will be working hard to accomplish your objective, which will probably involve *changing your partner's behavior,* not hypothetically but actually.

Go through the scene, speaking all your lines and sticking to the general outline of the action that you have been using. This time, as you work, try to create a real reaction in your partner. She will probably do many things just because they are specified in the script, but see if you can elicit a genuine response from her. (For example, your partner may have the line, "You scared me." She is going to say the line no matter what happens, and maybe even try to indicate that she is scared. See, however, if you can really surprise your partner, causing a bit of fright. If the scene calls for a romantic relationship, see if you can charm your partner. Seduce her.)

How will you do this? That is what your tactics are all about. Choose one approach to begin, and see if you can carry out your actions and deliver your lines so that your partner is changed. If you get even a small response, feel good and proceed. If not, after a few lines change tactics and see if something else works better. All the time your partner will be trying to do the same to you. The scene may heat up quite a bit in very short order.

This is an exploratory rehearsal. Not every moment will work immediately. It is enough if you get a bit of a response. You will know when you are on the right track. Don't get so busy pursuing your objective that you forget to stay open to your partner. Listen and observe as closely as possible to see what your partner is doing. Your scene is not a predetermined set of actions being lined up and nailed in like planks, but a free improvisation within the framework of the script's lines and directions. Both you and your partner are learning what works and doesn't work.

After this run-through, it might be useful to talk about it a little. Don't tell your partner what to do or judge his performance. Just say what affected you: *When you jumped out from behind the door, I really felt frightened.* Identify the two or three most powerful reactions you had, listen while your partner does the same, and then move on.

You will probably have time for several repetitions. Explore different tactics each time you go through the scene. Gather as much information as you can about what will work and what won't. In later rehearsals you will want to develop consistency, but at this stage you want to discover all you can about the scene. Remember to keep choosing your actions anew each time you do them. Don't allow the scene to sink into routine. After each run-through, do a quick debriefing about what was especially effective at changing you and your partner.

This rehearsal will give you immense amounts of information about the scene, about your partner, and about your abilities. Don't be surprised if the relationship between the characters in the scene deepens and their exchanges intensify: the structure on the page is beginning to come to life. The idea is to learn ways to fulfill the play's imperatives, which you do by bringing life to the objectives and tactics. The social exchange is paramount here.

You will have scripts in your hands throughout this rehearsal, which may be inhibiting. That's fine: you are still a long way from performance. Don't surrender to old habits of symbolic behavior, however. Keep choosing your actions. Keep trying to actually change your partner's behavior. Keep trying to achieve your objective even though you may be going slowly and checking the text often.

Take a minute at the end of this rehearsal to make a few notes to yourself in the margins of your script about what worked and what new ideas you may have had about the scene. Let your partner know how much you enjoyed the work.

In between Step 4 and Step 5
You may very likely already know your script by heart at this point, but if you don't, now is the time to learn your lines. Use the techniques you used when preparing your monologue. Go over them until they are secure. Think through the scene and identify any additional props you may need. Locate those final pieces. Start thinking about what you will wear. You don't need to go out and purchase a nurse's uniform or a pair of cowboy boots, but think about what you have in your wardrobe that will give you a tactile feeling of being the character and the audience an idea of the ambience of the play. Wear the closest thing you have to what the play calls for.

If there's time, read the entire play again to remind you of the big picture. The details of rehearsal can narrow your vision. Try to recapture a sense of the whole. Finally, look back over your notes from the analysis work to reacquaint yourself with the objectives and as-ifs of your character. Knowing what you now know about the scene, are they still appropriate? Can you strengthen them?

Step 5: Layering on the verbal level
In the first rehearsal of the scene with your partner, you worked to build the sensory foundation. This is the largest section of your thought and needs the most attention: you are creating the given circumstances and entering into them by using the "magic if." In the second rehearsal you maintained that foundational sensory layer

while adding social interaction with your partner. Much of that rehearsal focused on learning to have interactions with your partner that grow out of the sensory layer rather than displace it. The emphasis was on changing your partner's behavior, an interaction that you monitored using your senses.

This third rehearsal focuses on adding the verbal layer to the previous layers without overriding them. Today your attention will often be on the words of the scene, but make sure to double-check that you make the shift to the creative state and that you maintain it. Verbal work has a tendency to trigger the logical mind. If this happens, focus for a brief time on the sensory and interrelational parts of the scene until you feel the mental shift back to where you want to be.

Begin this rehearsal by setting up your space. Take the first fifteen minutes to do a warm-up, concluding with a see-and-be-seen exercise or a sensory exploration.

Sitting knee to knee with your partner, go through the memorized lines of the scene. You may have the script with you, but try not to use it. This should feel just like the first time you read the scene with your partner in this knee-to-knee arrangement, only this time you won't have to look down at the text for each line, since you have already memorized it. If you cannot remember your next line, don't panic. Before looking at the text, take a second to relax your muscles and take a deep breath. Ninety percent of all memory lapses are associated with simple oxygen deprivation. We get a bit tense, hold our breath, and brain function slows down. After you take a breath, the line often pops into your head. Reestablish eye contact and continue.

If the scene does not go particularly smoothly the first time through (not unusual), repeat the exercise to help familiarize yourself with the words. Don't be surprised if you find that remembering the lines is harder than you thought it would be. Seek to maintain good eye contact with your partner. Don't recite the words, but choose them—mean them—every time you say them.

During the final half hour, you want to do essentially this same thing, but on your feet, moving through the actions of the scene. Run the scene, the first time with your script in hand but consulting it as little as possible. Never just say a line. Instead, stay connected to your physical creation of the given circumstances, which includes your relationship to your partner. Pursue your objectives fully. If something has to suffer a little, let it be the lines rather than your actions.

We all have the native ability to do each of the steps of performing. We have done them all in isolation. What tends to go wrong in beginners' performances is that each successive layer of work completely supplants and replaces the previous layers. Actors do great work on given circumstances, and then throw it away to concentrate on the relationship. They get the relationship going strongly, but then forget about it because they are trying to recall their lines. The job here is to keep layering the new steps onto the old, not letting anything get away. This requires time and patience, which is why we rehearse.

After running the scene once on your feet, set your script down and see what you can do. In the best of situations very little attention goes to the lines. You just "know" what the next line is without mentally disengaging to "look it up" somewhere in your head. Most of your concentration is on the sensory and interpersonal aspects of the scene. You are paying attention to what is happening now, not living in your mind.

After the run-through, take a moment to talk about what your partner is doing that is succeeding in changing you—the things you are not having to pretend, because they are really happening to you. Listen carefully while your partner does the same. Limit your conversation to just that one topic, and avoid the negatives. There's no need to dwell on what isn't working. You both know.

Take a second to consult your script about any specific problems. Do you always have trouble with one particular line? Look it up and think about it for a minute. We usually can't remember a line because we don't understand *why* we say it. Look at the script again to see the line's connection to the previous material.

You will probably have time to run through the scene two or three more times. Enjoy the unspoken agreements you and your partner are making. There is little need for discussion, but notice how much is being suggested and acted on through nonverbal communication.

If the scene isn't going quite as you hoped (and it frequently doesn't), try to influence your partner's behavior through your tactics during the next run of the scene. Be so interesting, clever, and forceful that your partner instinctively responds in the way you want; don't fall back on suggesting what to do.

It is common for this rehearsal to feel a bit discouraging. The addition of the verbal layer as memorized text is apt to slow progress down, and sometimes even cause a bit of backsliding. Don't let it get you down if it feels like less ground is covered in this rehearsal than in your previous ones. Though there may be fewer discoveries about the scene, you are building the layers up in a way that will serve you later. At the end of the rehearsal, go out of your way to let your partner know that you appreciate the collaboration. Everyone likes a little praise, especially when the going gets tough.

In between Step 5 and Step 6

A lot of work is now beginning to happen in your subconscious. You will often find yourself thinking about the scene away from rehearsals. New ideas may pop into your head without your even realizing you were thinking about the scene.

There are two specific jobs to do before the next rehearsal.

The first is to reread the scene, paying special attention to its humor. Look for the light touch and the odd perspective. This is not the same as jokes or overt silliness. The scene may not be comic, but there are ways we all bring a special twist to everything we do to keep from being overwhelmed by the pressures of everyday living. Look to see how your character does this. The more serious the scene, the more important this is.

The second is to think about what happens just before the scene begins and just after it ends. Your acting needs to begin offstage, out of the audience's sight. To do this you need to invent a minute or so of your character's life before the scene begins. This is true even if you are beginning with the first lines of the printed scene, not just if you are picking it up in the middle. The scene doesn't begin at the point you step across the threshold. Your character has a life on the other side of the door as well. Find and discover it. Look at two or three possibilities about how you can enter the scene.

Likewise, the scene doesn't end for your character when you finish your last line. Instead, imagine the character's future thoroughly enough that you could continue the performance for one full minute. You'll never actually do this bit of the scene, but your acting will stay powerful up until the word *curtain*.

> *Q: When you're in a show, what's the last thing you do before you go on?*
> *A: It changes from play to play. You are hunting for that thing that your character has done before he gets into the place you're going to. It's amazing how the backstage environment will accommodate that.*
> *—Anthony Zerbe, interviewed by Don Shewey*

If there are any missing elements to the scene—sound effects, props, etc.—that have not been attended to, now is the time.

Step 6: Steering the performance
Having undertaken the first three stages of the pyramid, this rehearsal is the one in which you will most fully concentrate on integrating the logical layer.

Begin this rehearsal with a warm-up and an exercise to get into the creative state. Take special care to set up the environment fully. Add any new props. If any elements require a third person's help—a sound effect, for example—ask your helper to attend this rehearsal and integrate his contribution at the appropriate spot.

You will have forty-five minutes or so to run the scene several times. You will have a chance to incorporate your decisions about what is happening just before and after the scene and to include the humor you discovered.

This is also the rehearsal in which you must incorporate overt physical interactions (such as fighting or kissing) into the scene. The rule of thumb is simple: the person who seems to be the recipient of the action on stage is actually controlling the action. It is the kissee, not the kisser, who choreographs this moment. It is the "victim" of the violence who determines the actions and the sequence of events. You don't want anyone to get hurt or to feel taken advantage of. Putting the initiative in the hands of the person who is the recipient of the action on stage helps prevent this.

You may be able to bring in an expert to show you some stage combat techniques or choreograph a dance or a similar patterned activity. If you do, remember that the cue for the action to begin in the scene is always the responsibility of the recipient. Until that person is ready, nothing goes forward.

Most of today's rehearsal is about being sure that everything you are choosing in the scene is in pursuit of your objectives. Seek your desires powerfully. Notice what keeps you from having them, be it your partner's actions, something in the given circumstance, or some inability on your character's part. These are traditionally called *the obstacles*. At this stage, it is important to know not only what you want, but what prevents you from getting it.

This is the process of *alignment*—seeing that all your acting skills are serving the narrative of the text. By this stage in rehearsal you will note that many things are beginning to fall into a pattern. One tactic consistently works with your partner. One action in the script begins to have reliable timing. Now is the time to check to see that things aren't becoming rote or routine, and that it's all appropriate to the text.

There is no magic method to this. Just think about these problems as you proceed. Run the scene several times, making sure your objectives are appropriate and that you achieve them.

Your next rehearsal, which will be your last, should be held in the space in which you are going to perform. If you've been rehearsing elsewhere up to now, make sure you and you partner know who's moving what to the new space. Thank your partner and any assistants for a good rehearsal and adjourn.

In between Step 6 and Step 7

Before final dress rehearsal gather everything you will need and make a short checklist. There will be a lot to remember on the day of performance. To keep from forgetting something in the confusion, organize now.

Look back over the script and double-check your lines. Be sure that you are speaking the exact words the author set down for you.

Try to focus your thoughts on the given circumstances and the "magic if." Let your mind freely fantasize about the sensory conditions of the scene, instead of worrying about the outcome of the performance.

Step 7: The dress rehearsal

At the final rehearsal you have only a few specific jobs to accomplish and a lot of things to enjoy. Before you do anything else, set the scene up in the performance space. Discuss with your partner where the audience should be in relation to the scene. If your scene takes place in a room, for example, discuss which one of its four walls the audience should "watch" it through. That is, decide which angle provides the best viewing for the audience, and arrange the furniture to face that way. (Too often scenes happen on a generic "stage living room." You were earlier instructed about how to avoid this by arranging a real room, instead of a hopelessly stagey one.) Don't adjust any more than is absolutely necessary for the performance.

If your performance is not part of a class or an event, you will need to decide whom to invite and arrange for someone to greet and seat them. (Don't do this yourself.) For record-keeping purposes, you will want to have your performance videotaped. Discuss with your partner who will do the taping and how you will each get a copy of the final tape.

Change into the clothing you will wear in the scene. It is very important that you do this in this rehearsal, even if the clothes are delicate or need to be kept clean. You must be sure that everything you have planned is possible *before* the performance. Don't leave anything out of this rehearsal. It is just like a performance.

Set up the props and all the materials you will need. Run the scene several times, including any introduction you plan to give. (This is traditionally a brief announcement of the title of the play the scene is from, its author, and the names of the performers.) If the end of the scene is not being indicated technically (lights fading out, a curtain coming down), then say the word *curtain*.

Each time you go through the scene be sure to recommit yourself to acting it fully. You are practicing the simultaneous creation of all the layers. Induce the creative state. Create the given circumstances. Invest in the relationship, and choose your actions. Speak in a fully realized manner, not from rote memory. Pursue your character's objectives with the intent to change your partner's behavior. Align your performance with the intentions of the playwright.

When you have finished, you are done for the day. Thank your partner for the productive rehearsal period and turn your attention to the performance.

Performance

Rehearsing and performing are different, but never as different as in the actor's frame of mind. Rehearsal is careful, slow, sequential thought. It is building the performance through layers of work. It involves critical thinking and judgment of the steps as you go. Performance is not at all like that.

Performance thinking is freewheeling, wholistic, and energizing. It is the gestalt of theatre, a form of thought carried out mainly below the layers of our consciousness. To explore this a bit, let's revisit the example of gestalt thought given in Chapter 3: driving on the freeway, we synthesize an enormous amount of complex data but are almost unaware of our "thoughts" when carrying it out. Driving doesn't feel anything like learning to drive did. Learning was slow, difficult, and complicated. Doing the job now, however, is simple— often a pleasure.

Performing your scene will be like this. All the work of rehearsal is behind you. The lines will be there when you need them, but you will not have to "go get" them. You'll just know them. You won't have any trouble recalling your actions. These will come as second nature. In rehearsal you needed to try many things, choose the most effective, constantly prepare and revise. In performance, you will not have to do any of those things. You will just do it.

> *The brain is a good stagehand. It gets on with its work while we're busy acting out our scenes.*
> —Diane Ackerman

In performance your mind will be on only what is happening in the present moment. You will attend to the sights and sounds, and especially to the actions and reactions of your partner, but you won't have to think about what is going on with your lines, actions, strategies, or emotions. These things will take care of themselves. (More accurately, you will be taking care of them, but on the subconscious rather than on the conscious level.)

After the best performances, actors often cannot recall exactly what they did. They will have near perfect recall of their partners' actions and many peripheral details but not even a glimmer of what they themselves did.

How will you know if your performance is good? It will *feel* good. You will have a literal feeling, a sensation, of accomplishment and of well-being. You will feel the way you felt after being deeply immersed in the sensory exploration exercise.

If that is the goal, how will you get there? Prepare carefully for your performance. Make sure you are performing on adequate rest and nutrition. Once you get to the performance site, set up the stage, paying particular attention to the props. Use the checklist you created earlier to assure yourself that everything you need is where it should be. (Double-check to see that the videotaping equipment is ready and the person who will tape your scene is there.) Walk the scene through once, by yourself, going over your lines and actions. Change into your performance clothes, and then put the scene from your mind. You have done all you could to prepare, and everything is ready.

> *I am aware that now I'm working in very nonlinear ways. I am aware that I'm working now even when I don't think I'm working. In large part that's because there's so much of myself that has become trustworthy.*
> —Olympia Dukakis

The final step: Performance

Warm up to prepare your voice and body. With your partner, or on your own, do an exercise to help you make the transition to the creative state.

Make sure you have arranged the day so that you have no further responsibilities until performance time. Avoid distractions now until you begin. Be sure the scene is introduced as it was in rehearsal, by you or by your partner. (It is theatrical courtesy for the performer who speaks second in the scene to introduce it. This gives the performer who speaks first an extra second or two to prepare.) Go offstage to prepare.

Remember that your performance is going to begin in the wings, before you come into view. It takes only a few seconds to prepare yourself. Take a deep breath and focus your attention on something small, perhaps a prop in your hands like a glass or a paper. If it is imperative that your hands be empty when you enter, use a small item like a key that you can slip into your pocket as you enter. Use the item in your hands to help you renew your creative state of mind. When that has happened, slowly expand your circle of attention until it encompasses your whole body and, ultimately, the backstage area in which you are waiting.

With your attention on the physical environment, make your entrance. Connect with your partner as quickly as the scene allows. Attend carefully to what your partner is doing and to how he or she is responding to what you are doing. All else will take care of itself. Play the performance. If anything goes awry, incorporate it into the scene. Pick up the fallen hats, mop up the spills, but *do so as your character.* If you should have a sudden memory lapse, remember to breathe deeply. The odds are that the situation is temporary and a little oxygen will correct it. If you don't signal your panic, there is a good chance that the audience will not notice. That's it. Allow the scene to soar. Trust that everything you need will be there for you, and enjoy the process.

Student Portraits

Dan and Lynn

All the members of the group were working on final scenes. Many were going smoothly through the rehearsal process, but there were a few hiccoughs. Dan and his partner, Lynn, were having trouble finding a time they could get together. Both worked full-time. Dan was a student at a local college. Lynn was married with small children. Neither had much free time. The issue was not whether either of them was willing to put in the time needed to prepare the scene. They were both excited and motivated. It was just that at first glance their schedules seemed mutually exclusive.

At the advice of the instructor they both brought in their calendars and shared their schedules. Dan laughed and rolled his eyes. He had not really understood the complications in Lynn's schedule. Especially in the late afternoon, his preferred rehearsal time, she had an incredibly tight set of commitments mostly having to do with picking up one child after school and getting him delivered to his next lesson or activity by the time another child was arriving home from her school by bus. Dan was committed to his job for six evenings a week and had to be back at college for classes early the next morning, Lynn's preferred time. Both discovered only one likely time in their schedules—weekend afternoons when Lynn's husband could baby-sit and Dan had not yet reported to work. They agreed to meet both Saturday and Sunday, though they would have preferred a schedule that placed one of the rehearsals in midweek.

Will and Amy

At first Will and Amy seemed to be doing great, but by the second week the process had ground almost to a halt. Will confided to the instructor that something was going terribly wrong, but he didn't know what it was. Approaching Amy, the instructor discovered the problem. Amy had grown quite unsure of Will's extratheatrical intentions.

The problem came up when Will had suggested a couple of scene possibilities that involved strong romantic relationships between the characters. In the end they had chosen something less passionate, and it seemed that Will had never sensed Amy's concern. She, in turn, suspected that maybe he had more in mind than scene work.

Unfortunately, the problems compounded when Will volunteered his apartment as a rehearsal site. Once again, the two missed each other's intentions. Will did not, in the opinion of the instructor, really intend anything more than the convenience of using a place to which he knew he always had access. Amy, however, was anxious about spending her evenings alone in a single man's apartment and was concerned about what Will intended.

This problem required some good, honest communication between the two to solve. Amy was uncomfortable, and Will was insensitive to her discomfort.

With the instructor present, a rehearsal was held in which it became possible for Amy to confess that she was having trouble being this emotionally open and honest with someone without implying a romantic intention. She expressed why she thought maybe Will was intending to use the scene to start a personal relationship with her. Will was hurt and angry, feeling accused of a serious transgression of both morals and ethics.

This was no small problem, but it was possible for the instructor to help both see that it is important to make a separation between the scene and life. In this case it was important also to set some ground rules to keep everyone comfortable.

Amy asked, and Will agreed, that rehearsals take place in a semi-public place rather than alone in Will's apartment. It turned out that Will had no real agenda for suggesting his home, and he saw the point in selecting a place that seemed more businesslike. (Ironically, the scene did take place in a living room. Most of Will's furniture was eventually used, including the hide-a-bed couch he slept on every night, but he admitted that he could see why it felt a lot different to use it in the theatre.) Amy, for her part, agreed to be more forthcoming if she had any problems with arrangements, rather than let her fears get the best of her. She did set a couple of limits (including how late she was willing to rehearse) that bothered Will a bit, but he agreed to live with them. This scene recovered in ways that many never do from such misunderstandings, however, because both grew more sensitive to some of the issues underlying their initial difficulties. More open communication and more thought about avoiding the appearance of threatening circumstances helped a lot.

Tim and Susan

Tim and Susan selected a very powerful scene from a contemporary play that included a great deal of stage combat. At one point in the scene Susan's character knees Tim's character in the crotch. Later in the scene, partially to make up, she kisses his face and hands. Both had said that they were "scared out of their wits" about the scene. They thought it was great material—very dramatic and literate—but they didn't know if they would be up to it. The instructor congratulated them on having the courage to attempt the scene. It was a good one, and they were brave to choose it rather than go for something safe and easy.

In the third rehearsal, a friend of the instructor's with lots of stage combat experience came in to help choreograph. He laughingly observed that early in his career he never dealt with scenes with this dynamic. "It was always men beating up women back then," he said. "And kissing them, too. The woman never initiated. Now things have changed. It's more fun now that plays aren't so sexist and predictable."

He arranged the combat, and the romance, so that Tim was turned away from the audience slightly and could not be seen blinking his eyes to tell Susan that he was ready to begin. The fight choreographer showed them a way to stage the fight so it looked real but didn't involve danger to either person. (Tim later confessed that in one rehearsal he had lost his concentration and blinked to Susan that he was ready before he really was. Fortunately, the stunt was designed in an almost foolproof way, so Tim didn't pay for his mistake too severely. Still he said he wished he had learned on the kiss instead of the kick.)

Robert and Laurie

Robert and Laurie found a scene that both had loved from the beginning, despite the fact that the characters were quite unlike them. Robert's character in the play, as a matter of fact, was of a completely different ethnicity, as well as being temperamentally different. Laurie's very quirky and slightly silly character was also quite a stretch for her.

The rehearsal process was very exciting for both. Just pursuing the objectives had led each of them to characterizations that were markedly different from their own personalities. Robert, especially, was very good at seeing the world through his character's eyes. The level of his transformation was astonishing.

By the midpoint of rehearsal Laurie was finding that she was having some trouble. She could adopt her character's viewpoint but not quite capture her rhythm. At the instructor's suggestion she experimented with thinking of the character's body and tempo as part of the given circumstances. What if her character had a different walk, a different speed of expression, or a different accent? She experimented with all three, finding that experimenting with the character's tempo helped her find a whole new persona.

Winding Up

The group had come to the end of their time together. They decided to celebrate their accomplishments by having a party. Some of them were going on to more formal training, some were pursuing amateur opportunities, a few were content to have had the experience without wanting to go any further. Because the main thing they now had in common was their enjoyment of the time together, they decided that a final party should be a congratulatory bash instead of a maudlin good-bye. At Kim's suggestion, each person in the class hung a large piece of brown paper on the wall. Everyone in the group went around the room and wrote a compliment or a congratulatory message on each person's paper. In addition to their new skills, each had a pleasant reminder of the experience to take home.

Journal Entry: Rehearsals and Performances

Many actors keep a journal throughout their careers. In it, they make brief notes about what happened at each rehearsal and each performance. These notes usually cover what material was rehearsed or performed, the specific goals of the rehearsal, what actually happened, and any observations about things learned or questions still unanswered.

For this scene, do the same. You do not need to keep elaborate notes, but write down when and where you rehearsed, for how long, what you hoped to accomplish in the rehearsal, and what actually happened.

After the performance, avoid negative self-analysis (the scene never goes as well as we dream in our heart of hearts) but do try to detail what things you accomplished. What skills did you employ for the first time? What worked (if only for a second or two)? What would you still like to try if you could do the scene again? How have you grown since you began to study? Focus less on audience reception than on how you felt during the performance. You will use these sensations to guide you in the future. Start your life's journal now.

Resources

Selecting Material

This is a book about learning an acting *process*. It is important that you select material that contributes to your learning how to act, which is quite different than selecting material for public performance or for audition. For that reason, the guidelines for selecting material that follow are about helping you find selections appropriate for the *learning* process. Only in rare cases will you be performing a complete theatrical piece as an exercise or for your class. Usually you will be working with short sections of longer plays. It is not important to learning the process of acting that these tell a complete story for the benefit of an audience. (In this regard, these guidelines differ somewhat from those for selecting material for auditions, which appear later in this section.)

Material selection is, for most actors-in-training, the most difficult part of their class. Without a lot of experience with the resources available to help locate appropriate literature, many actors find themselves settling for material about which they don't know much and that they sometimes don't actually like. This section is designed to discuss the major issues involved in choosing pieces and to point you toward sources of material. It will help you find challenging, engaging, and appropriate pieces.

Before we do anything else, a vital distinction must be made. Unless otherwise instructed, it is imperative that you learn to tell the difference between dramatic and nondramatic material, and work only with the former. Dramatic material is written in the form of character's speech. It is designed for use in the theatre. Dramatic material includes plays (written for the stage), screenplays (for movies), and teleplays (for television). It is easily discerned because, except for a few stage directions, it consists of characters' speeches. You can recognize them instantly because each speech is preceded by a speech heading, which is the name of the character who will say the words. Here is a very short dialogue in this form:

> NINA: I'm just crazy about you.
> KONSTANTIN: We're alone.
> NINA: Is that someone over there?
> KONSTANTIN: No, nobody. (*He kisses her*)

Nondramatic material consists of narrative prose from novels, newspapers, and other sources that is designed to be read silently. It may contain dialogue, quotation, and other forms of characters' speech, but there will be no speech headings. Instead, you will see qualifiers buried inside the prose to credit the speaker. It looks like this:

> "It is very hot out here today," Daryl said absently. Diane looked up at him and dismissively answered, "I know. I can feel it without assistance."

This material can be deceiving, because it looks like it is performable, but it is designed for a reader, not an actor. Until you are more familiar with what might work in the theatre, avoid this kind of selection. Poetry is also nondramatic material. It is generally to be avoided as well.

The next few pages address some frequently asked questions about material selection.

Defining Monologues

What is a monologue? The exercises in this book call for you to prepare one short solo piece, called a monologue. *Monologue* literally means "solo talk." It is a selection from a play in which you are the sole speaker, and in which you are playing one consistent character. Most monologues are short sections edited from a one-act or full-length play where the character you will be portraying speaks for an uninterrupted stretch of time to a silent listener. (Characters inside plays sometimes speak at length to themselves or to the audience. This is called *soliloquy* and though this material technically fits our definition, it isn't recommended. Soliloquies are usually designed to fill the audience in on background exposition or to make literary transitions in plays and as a general rule don't make good work material.) A monologue, therefore, is one actor playing one character who is speaking to someone else without interruption.

How long should my monologue be? Instructors have differing preferences on this, so if you have one be sure to clarify her exact criterion, but monologues generally come in one of two standard lengths: (1) close to, but under, sixty seconds or (2) no less than ninety seconds but no more than two minutes. The former guideline is common in large classes, in situations where you will (eventually) be performing two monologues back-to-back, or where the piece will get double use as a standard audition. The longer format is typical in classes of ten students or less, in situations where the piece is used exclusively for classroom exercises, or in situations where it might get double use as a graduate school audition piece. *Most beginning students vastly underestimate the amount of time it takes to perform their chosen piece* and consequently select material that is considerably too long for the specified format. Time your potential selections by reading them aloud, not silently, and plan for your monologue to take additional time once it is acted. Read aloud at a normal pace, a monologue that times in at forty-five seconds will take about one minute to perform. A ninety-second reading will yield a two-minute monologue. It is better to be too short than too long.

What should I look for in terms of content? Three things: First, look for a piece in which the character is *showing*, not *telling*. You want a piece that is active, in which a character is doing something and changing on the spot, not just telling about the past or about what happened to another character. Second, look for a piece that you can perform as written. The monologue is the artistic creation of the playwright, not our personal property. If you don't like the vocabulary of the character, or it expresses an idea you oppose, you don't have to perform it, but you can't change it. (Many high school students work in situations where they are explicitly instructed to change obscenities and blasphemy to milder euphemisms, but this is technically illegal and artistically unethical. Perform the piece or not, but don't alter it to suit your taste.) Finally, look for a piece that is about ideas and actions that engage you. Be fearless about trying new things, but stay away from "safe" material. In the end it won't sustain your interest. In the classroom it is not necessary that your piece tell a complete story or end in a theatrically satisfying way, but most students find it easier to work with material that has a clear beginning, middle, and end.

Can I use any dramatic material as a source for my monologue?
Unless your instructor specifically issues other criteria, the standard
guideline in most beginning acting classrooms is to select from
contemporary realistic plays. (The reasons for concentrating on
realism are explained in Chapter 1.) In addition, contemporary
plays are apt to provide current, relevant material that is not overexposed. In my own classroom, I ask my students not to perform
selections from plays written before they were born, in part because
I have grown weary of repeatedly seeing the same Tennessee Williams
and Neil Simon pieces, however interesting they may intrinsically
be to the first-time reader. I am not alone among theatre people in
this opinion. Instructors have varying feelings about selections
from current film and television. The advantage of choosing from
these sources is that you may be more familiar with them than
with current plays and because of the Internet, you may have more
access to them. The disadvantage is that a specific performance
may be in your head and the temptation to imitate it, as opposed to
creating your own version, can be overwhelming. The default guideline, in lieu of other instruction, is to stick to theatrical selections.
Suggestions of specific titles and sources of material appear later in
this section, which may make it easier to find theatrical titles for the
unfamiliar.

What kind of character should I play? This is the most complicated question of all. A longer section on the issues of representation appears later in this appendix, but for now the down-and-
dirty guideline common to the greatest number of beginning acting
classrooms is to select from characters that are fundamentally like
you. Selecting characters that are approximately your same age,
gender, ethnicity, and temperament lets you concentrate on the
process of acting without being distracted by having to research a
character's qualities lying outside your own experience. Having
said that, I would qualify by noting that many of the surface characteristics specified for the *dramatis personae* are simply default
choices without much meaning. There is a tendency to assign male
gender, Caucasian ethnicity, middle age, and heterosexual orientation to characters as generic characteristics. My personal experience
in the classroom is that especially my female students, gay and les-
bian students, and students from any descent other than western
European can widen the number of pieces available for their consideration by taking into account the real importance (or lack of

importance) of the gender, orientation, and ethnic description assigned to characters. In many cases, especially with professional characters like doctors and lawyers, there is no particular reason for assuming these are all straight white males and no reason to restrict who plays them. I now issue my general guideline to my own classes in this way: if it is important to play the character as being of an age, gender, ethnicity, or sexual orientation differing highly from your own, and the essential aspects of that difference lie outside your personal experience, save this material for later in your artistic development and seek something closer to home for your initial exercises. If these aspects of the character are not important to defining whom the character is, have a field day!

Monologue checklist

In the absence of modified guidelines from your instructor, these parameters can serve as selection criteria. Your monologue should be:

From a contemporary realistic play.

Of appropriate length (between sixty and ninety seconds).

Active: showing, not telling.

Addressed to a silent listener, not a soliloquy to an audience.

Performable as written.

Spoken by a character whose age, gender, and ethnicity are similar to your own.

Defining Scenes

What is a scene? As opposed to a monologue, a scene is a dialogue (a "duo talk") between two (or occasionally three) characters. Like monologues, scenes are short sections edited from one-act or full-length plays, but involving two or more active characters. The dialogue ordinarily alternates between characters rather than consists of long back-to-back monologues. In good classroom scenes the amount of dialogue assigned to each character is relatively balanced in both length and importance of content. (By the way, nothing so quickly marks you as a novice as calling your scenes *skits*. In theatrical circles, the word *skit* has very negative connotations of amateurism and vapidity.)

How long should my scene be? Differing instructors have differing preferences on this also, but a standard length is five minutes. The outside limit is ten minutes, though it is a rare instructor that prefers the longer type.

What should I look for in terms of content? Just as in the monologues, it is best to look for a scene in which the characters are actively doing something, rather than just talking to each other. If the scene contains combat of some kind, you might want to consult your instructor to see if some guidance will be available in safely executing these maneuvers before settling on this material.

Can I use any dramatic material as a source for my scene? The same guidelines used in defining the parameters of the material for your monologue will most likely apply to your scene. It is especially worth clarifying whether or not you may use material from films and television before investing time in finding this material.

What kind of character should I play? Again, the same guidelines will probably apply to character choice for a scene as applied to your monologue selection.

Scene checklist
In the absence of modified guidelines from your instructor, these parameters can serve as selection criteria. Your scene should be:

From a contemporary realistic play.

Of appropriate length (five minutes is the default format).

Active: showing, not telling.

Performable as written.

Spoken by a character whose age, gender, and ethnicity are similar to your own.

Where to Look for Material
Once you know the parameters for selecting materials, you still need to know where to locate possibilities for pieces. There is a great deal of material available, but unfortunately many young actors fall back on the few older plays that appear widely on high school reading lists with which they are already familiar.

It is a good plan to look for exciting, contemporary material when selecting scenes and monologues. If you are in a class, your instructor will appreciate seeing interesting, new titles. As a starting point for reading plays, familiarize yourself with recent winners of the Pulitzer prize for drama and other works by authors who have won this award. Recent winners include Nilo Cruz, Suzan-Lori Parks, David Auburn, Donald Margulies, Margaret Edson, Paula Vogel, Horton Foote, Edward Albee, and Tony Kushner. Add to this list winners of the Tony award for best play, like Richard Greenberg and August Wilson, and you will have a very good beginning list.

A favorite resource among advanced theatre students is *American Theatre* magazine, published by the Theatre Communications Group (TCG). This superb periodical regularly publishes new plays and translations that are cutting-edge and come with insightful interviews with authors alongside the text of the plays. Academic libraries are apt to carry back issues in bound volumes. The latest edition is probably available on your neighborhood newsstand.

When glancing through a complete play looking for extractable excerpts for monologues, be aware that the opening speeches of acts tend to be exposition. They look long enough but may be more talk than action. Longer speeches imbedded inside scenes are better bets. It may take a bit of editing to eliminate a word or two of superfluous response from an otherwise silent partner to get the piece into monologue form.

While in the bookstore looking for *American Theatre*, check the theatre aisle for further sources. Even in relatively small towns booksellers are apt to stock a large collection of books containing scenes and monologues especially designed for use in acting classes. The best of these are collections edited from recent stage plays and are apt to contain both scenes and monologues. Flip open the cover and look at the table of contents. A standard format for these collections divides selections into useful categories: monologues for men, monologues for women, scenes for two men, scenes for two women, and scenes for one man and one woman. Look at the index to see that the collection contains material from several authors. Check the copyright page to see the year the book was published. It is likely to contain copyright notices on the selections inside, so you can get an idea of the age of individual pieces at the same time. The best of these collections provide an introduction to each piece telling the basic plot of the play. Scene and monologue books are meant to give you an introduction to a great deal of literature at one time, but they do not substitute for reading the complete play. Once you have chosen a piece, look into finding the entire script. If you attend a college or university, ask if the theatre department has a script-lending library. You will also find more specialized collections of these books, with titles like *Monologues for Women of Color* and *Scenes for Teens*. If you cannot find these easily in your area, a quick trip to your favorite online book source, like *Amazon.com,* will yield a plethora of possibilities by typing in the words "monologues" and "scenes" into the search function.

Somewhat more suspect with instructors are books of scenes and monologues written especially for classes. These are not excerpts from plays, but short performance pieces designed for class usage. The best of these contain a large number of selections by many different authors. Because these are not excerpts from plays, they are not tested in the theatre the way that the previous category is, and not all of them are good, but some are interesting original pieces by well-known authors that have never quite blossomed into full plays. (Facing the inevitability of the appearance of favoritism, I confess that I am actually quite fond of, and use, a series of these books published by the company that prints this book, Heinemann. You can find out more about these for yourself by consulting its website at *Heinemanndrama.com.*)

The least acceptable alternative of this sort is books of monologues and scenes written especially for classes by a single author. These tend to have a bland uniformity to all the pieces along with a melodramatic tone. I don't recommend them, but you should be aware of them because of their ubiquity at the bookstore. You can look through an example and make your own decision about its quality.

In recent years, vast amounts of material have become available on the Internet. Though the price is right, you must exercise great caution in sorting through this material. Individuals have posted this at their whim, and there is little quality control. These theatrical monologues and original plays tend to be apprentice work by frustrated, unpublished writers. Cinematic material is a better bet. Presuming that your instructor has indicated a willingness to accept selections from screenplays and teleplays, you will find a surprisingly large collection is available online. The caveat here is that the source of much of this material is transcriptions prepared by individuals who were watching a videotape and typing dialogue as they played-and-paused their way through it. The accuracy is sometimes obsessively good, but be skeptical. Misspellings and capitalization errors are good clues that you have a poorly prepared piece on your hands. Look for a better version.

If you are considering using original material of your own, you should immediately ask your instructor (if you have one) if this will be acceptable before proceeding. Many, in fact most, do not allow you to use your own pieces. Even if you are the exception and your work as an author is of professional quality, which is not always the case, it is hard to separate your competing interests as an actor and as an author, and for that reason alone many teachers forbid it.

Familiarizing yourself with theatrical literature is very rewarding. Don't feel embarrassed if you don't know a lot about current theatre as you begin, but don't shy away from correcting this situation either. Well-read actors have many advantages over their less literate counterparts, and this is such an easy advantage to develop. You can readily read a complete play at a single sitting. Dig in and enjoy yourself.

One final note: The theatre is a very competitive business, which means you need all the friends you can get. As you read plays for possible scenes and monologues, consider passing along interesting material that is not right for you to friends and classmates whom it does suit. They'll be grateful for your lead and might well return the favor. You can never have too many connections.

Representation

Most acting discussions are conducted around topics of technique, but more and more the public issues surrounding acting have to do with the meaning of performance. What does it mean to undertake the acting process, and what are the implications of playing someone other than yourself? These considerations are conditioned by a less than admirable historic context. For a long time, who could perform on the stage was highly restricted. For centuries women were banned from acting in most parts of the world. Until rather recent times, well after World War II, the opportunities for actors of color were extremely limited, to the extent that there were few roles available requiring them to portray their own ethnicity, and even fewer roles allowing them to portray characters thought of as being "white." Caucasian actors played most characters, sometimes appearing heavily made-up as characters of other ethnic extractions. Because these portrayals were often more parody than realism, there was understandable objection that these actors were *mis*representing the characters.

Representation remains a contentious social issue without easy answers. Some activists believe that playing characters unlike yourself is a very important tool for creating understanding. It is walking a mile in someone else's shoes. Others feel exactly the opposite, that all pretense is misrepresentation. They'd prefer that characters be played only by actors of identical gender, sexual orientation, and ethnicity.

Within the theatrical community the issue has often settled at the more practical level of creating greater opportunity for actors from underrepresented minorities. Two nontraditional casting initiatives are in widespread usage to lessen exclusionary practices. The first of these is commonly known as color-blind casting, though it also applies to gender, sexual orientation, and even age. Under this system actors are cast solely on their abilities, and the conventions surrounding the performance are structured so that the audience is led to an understanding that these factors are irrelevant. At a theatre practicing color-blind casting you might find an African American man playing Hamlet, an Asian American man playing his father (the Ghost), and a Caucasian woman playing his mother, Gertrude. The genetic impossibilities of the situation are treated as unimportant and irrelevant. (The actors playing these roles are rarely related in any production, so the audience is called upon to "suspend disbelief" already. The issue in productions cast using this convention is only a matter of degree.) Kenneth Branagh's film version of *Much Ado About Nothing* used this approach to great effect.

When it involves gender switching, this type of casting is sometimes called gender-blind casting. It might result in Rosencrantz or Guildenstern being played by a female, whose gender the audience is again taught to essentially think of as irrelevant.

Conceptual casting has similar outcomes, but an entirely different underlying logic. In this case, the gender, ethnicity, sexual orientation, or age of the actor is mismatched to the traditional representation of the character in order to make a point. There have been many productions of *Romeo and Juliet* that have specifically cast the feuding families as being of different ethnicities to bring issues of racism to the forefront. A famous "photonegative" production of *Othello* cast Patrick Stewart in the title role while the entire rest of the cast was African American for the same reason. All-female productions of some of Shakespeare's militaristic history plays, like *Henry V*, have challenged the typical hawkish and heroic interpretations of these plays. What would happen to our perceptions of power and entitlement if a Latino were cast in the role of Superman in a new movie?

Either of these nontraditional methods leads to greater diversity within the cast, but the effect in production is likely to be quite different under the two formats. For this reason, there is no easy approach to controversies about representation. A savvy actor needs to be aware of the conventions around the performance in which he or she is participating and think about the reasons for casting. Probably the least acceptable alternative in our age is an unexamined defaulting to a predominantly traditional white male cast. While there is no hard-and-fast rule that can be used to sort through the issues of representation, it is certain that you will need to think carefully about what characters you play and how you represent them. Observe current theatrical practice carefully, and talk with your instructor and classmates about these issues, as they are important considerations.

Some Discussion Questions About Casting and Representation

The following questions might be helpful in sorting through issues of representation regarding performances you have seen or roles in which you are (or might be) cast:

What is the traditional casting of this role? Does this casting fit that mold or would it constitute nontraditional casting?

What aspects of the character's description are important to the plot and theme of the play, and which seem to be more arbitrary assignments?

In cases of nontraditional casting, is this a matter of color/gender-blind casting or is it conceptual casting? (That is, are we expected to ignore the race and gender of the actor, or is it being used to make a specific conceptual point?)

How do the conventions observed in, or proposed for, this production shape the audience perception of the casting?

What considerations led to this casting? Was the director specifically trying to create opportunities for actors from underrepresented backgrounds? Did the nature of the available casting pool lead to choices about the casting, or was it driven entirely by conceptual considerations? Is there a social point to this casting? Is there a thematic statement being made?

Does the casting of this show derive from the author's conception, or is the director modifying the original specifications in some way?

How does the casting emotionally affect you? Intellectually?

How was the casting received by the audience in general?

Auditioning

If you choose to pursue acting, vocationally or avocationally, sooner or later you will need to learn to audition. There is a wide variety of methods for selecting actors for roles, none of them entirely satisfactory. At colleges and universities, auditions for parts sometimes use a system of *cold readings* (actors reading from a script that they have not previously studied) and sometimes use interviews, but the most common format is a brief presentation of prepared monologues.

The conventions surrounding the presentation of these monologues are very rigid and differ from classroom presentations of monologues, where the object is to learn acting skills. This section will give you guidelines for selecting and preparing a piece that fulfills the expectations for a standard audition.

Begin by taking a bit of pressure off yourself. You need to know that no matter how good your audition is, it will have a limited effect on the outcome. Casting is not a matter of finding the "best" actor and placing him in the "best" part. It is a complex set of decisions about matching actors, all with idiosyncratic personalities, physical natures, and skills, with roles that call for specific characteristics. Even if you are subjectively "right" for a part, in order to be cast in the role you need to fit into an ensemble of other actors who are "right" for their parts. Imagine for a moment that you are auditioning for the role of Juliet. You may be a terrific performer, the most skilled person who auditions for the part. You may give a terrific audition, the best one the director sees that day. You may fit the director's preconception of the role, looking exactly like he pictures Juliet in his head. In the end, you may still not get the role because you are noticeably taller than his only viable candidate for Romeo. The role will go to someone Romeo can kiss without standing on a box, even if she is much less suited overall to the role than you are. Of course, it could all happen in reverse, and you could be the lucky person cast because you look better next to Romeo than several more experienced candidates. For your own peace of mind, you want to feel you did all you could do, but relax some. Auditions are not the be-all and end-all of casting.

So why are you auditioning in the first place? Auditions are a way for directors and casting agents to familiarize themselves with the available casting pool quickly. From your perspective, you are auditioning to introduce yourself, or to remind people who already know you that you are available for casting. In a standard, large-scale session, called by the depersonalizing term *cattle call audition,* those doing the auditioning will see a new actor every two minutes on average. They will make very quick decisions about your suitability for roles in this production based on how you look and how you present yourself. You may or may not get to actually perform your piece, but the maximum amount of time you will spend acting in one of these rapid-turnover calls is sixty seconds. (If you are auditioning for a musical, you sometimes get to throw in an additional thirty seconds of a song.) To the uninitiated it can be shocking how fast decisions are made on how little evidence.

The purpose of this type of audition, then, is to present *yourself* in the best possible package in the shortest amount of time. It is much more important that you play yourself well in your entrance, introduction, and performance than that you demonstrate a particular acting skill you have acquired. Before one second of your monologue takes place, you will need to set yourself apart from the crowd by demonstrating professionalism and confidence. For most of us, this is where the real acting challenge takes place. How do you do this? Mainly by bearing in mind that everything "counts." How you dress, how you enter, how you introduce yourself, how you prepare your piece and what you do when you are done performing give a far greater sense of command than your actual acting. Simply being prepared and being professional will set you above the crowd.

In an average audition, it would not be uncommon for one hundred candidates to audition for each available part. Of them, seventy-five to eighty will fall out of contention for reasons that have nothing to do with their performance. Some will appear in clothes that look like they have been slept in for a week. A director thinks twice about casting someone of dubious hygiene for a long, intimate rehearsal period. Several will tell the director *all* about how nervous they are, but promise to work hard to make up for this deficit. They will never get the chance. Others will offer excuses before ever beginning, usually that they are ill, and not to expect much from them. Some will turn diva before the auditors' eyes and proclaim that they have been kept waiting too long. Many will be underprepared, forgetting lines, starting over, making up words as they go along, or simply *ad-libbing*. All of these will be dismissed from consideration, if not literally interrupted and asked to leave.

This is all unfortunate, because the rules of auditioning, though unwritten are fairly simple, and easy to obey.

- Dress well, but simply. You want to look like yourself, not an overly decorated version of yourself, or a casually wrinkled version; just look your energetic best. (Student actors tend to underdress for most auditions. A colored T-shirt, jeans, and a backward baseball cap send the message that you don't care enough about this part to put on something clean for the audition. How much additional passion will you bring to the role? directors wonder.)
- Plan *and rehearse* a short, simple introduction. As naturally as possible, learn to say, "Hi, I'm [your name, said loudly and distinctly]. My piece is from [play] by [author]." You'd be astonished how many actors flub their introduction or unbelievably don't know what play their monologue is from or whom it is by.
- Perform a piece that is absolutely, unquestionably less than sixty seconds. A piece that makes an impression in forty-five seconds would be a welcomed rarity. (In auditions where there is a timekeeper, like competitive thespian society auditions, time is called on well over half of all performers before they finish their pieces, meaning of course that their pieces are too long!)
- Select a piece that starts with a bang. Decisions are being made quickly. Make an immediate impression.
- Do something in your piece. Nine out of ten audition pieces are "talking heads." That is, the actors are just standing there speaking. Their bodies are uninvolved. Be the tenth actor, who is physically involved, and you will be memorable.
- As you finish, no matter what you may be thinking or feeling, leave the impression that you are pleased with your perform-

ance. Smile and say thank you. Making a negative evaluation of your work in public doesn't fix anything if it didn't go well, and may fix an inaccurate judgment in the minds of your auditors if it was good and you are just too hard on yourself.
- Leave confidently.

Many of my students find it surprising that these "rules" have so little to do with the performance itself. If you bear in mind that the important point is to present yourself as a confident, committed, energetic actor, then there are a few more things that might be said about the conventions of audition pieces that would help you. Just remember the suggestions that follow are flexible and have less bearing on being selected than you might think.

- Unless your auditors already know you very well, play a character that is very like you. In the classroom you can afford to stretch yourself. In a sixty-second audition when you play roles far from your "type," you just come across as someone with little self-knowledge. This impression isn't helped any by the fact that there are lots of people auditioning that really don't have a clue about their type. At any given audition, auditors will be subjected to eighteen-year-old King Lears and 250-pound Juliets
- Don't do overexposed material, or material where the auditor will have a famous performance in mind with which to compare you. At every musical audition about one-third of the sopranos will sing, "I'm just a girl who can't say no," from *Oklahoma*. At every play audition, several young men will do a Matt Damon impression using pieces from *Good Will Hunting*.
- Select a piece where you use your acting skills. That is, find a monologue that is set in a rich sensory environment, where your character develops emotionally, and where you make active, interesting choices. Play strong given circumstances.
- If the piece is addressed to a silent listener, put that imaginary listener directly in front of you, so that you are facing your auditors. Don't, however, turn your auditors into your silent partner. It bothers them when they are called upon to act back to you. They want to watch you.
- Don't costume the piece, except extremely subtly, and don't use any actual props. This is probably the greatest change

from classroom monologues. You are the focus in an audition, not the spectacle. In auditions you are expected to create anything you need out of your imagination and thin air.

- There will be a chair available for you to use. Unless you have a very specific physical idea for the chair, my advice is *don't use it*. Most actors who sit are doing so because they don't know what to do with their bodies.

- Look for a monologue with an engaging first line, especially a powerful question. ("Ever kill somebody? Ever want to?" goes the opening of a favorite piece.) A powerful, energetic action is even better. Get attention immediately.

- The best auditions change emotion and mood dramatically. They start in one place and move to another in forty-five seconds. You'd be surprised how rarely this happens and how memorable it is when it does.

- Always rehearse your piece with an entrance, an introduction, a transition before you begin, and a simple "thank you" at the end.

- When actually auditioning, listen carefully to what is said to you. When directors like what they are seeing, they are apt to ask you a question or two. A surprisingly large number of actors leave the second they are done performing and don't hear the questions. Be alert and available for instructions.

- If asked to change anything about your audition, give it your best shot without worrying about why they want you to change or even the sensibility of doing so. Sometimes directors want to see your flexibility, and sometimes they are looking for a quality needed in the character they are trying to cast that makes no sense with the piece you are performing as a monologue. Don't worry about that, just do your best.

Once you have finished an audition, judge your work on how well you accomplished what you intended to do, not the casting outcome. You might seek some honest feedback from trusted professors or discerning friends occasionally, but you are your own best guide. Have faith in your own abilities.

One final note: You will learn more about auditioning from watching one full day of auditions from behind the desk than from performing a dozen of them. Once in a while, volunteer to assist at an audition with checking candidates in, running the logistics of the rehearsal room, stage managing, or anything that will get you where you can watch fifty to one hundred auditions in a row. You'll see immediately what directors see and understand how can you stand out.

Comedy

Stanislavski's original technique has proven itself effective again and again with dramatic realism. His more wholistic approaches to acting opened up the plays of Ibsen, Chekhov, Gorki, and other early realists. One long-standing criticism of the Stanislavski system, however, is that it is not effective for comedy. The usual comparison is to say that Stanislavski (or Strasberg, Meisner, Adler, or Hagen for that matter) understood realism but not comedy. This criticism is, in some sense, misguided. Many prominent comedians throughout the last century and into this new one have been trained in some variant of the Stanislavski system and used it throughout their work to great acclaim. Comedy, however, does deserve some special consideration within the context of this book and the acting systems it attempts to illuminate.

Comedy is not a style, like realism or symbolism, but a genre. Derived from the French root word for "type," *genre* is a designation of the kind of play a particular title is. In this sense, comedy and realism are not opposites. They are not directly comparable terms.

Comedy is a designation dating from the time of the Greeks. In ancient times comedies were very loose affairs filled with physical slapstick, witty sayings, obscene songs, and a general silliness that only occasionally had to do with a story line. The most highly visible form of comedy in our time (after stand-up comedy, which is not a theatrical form) is the television situation comedy—the sitcom—which is a direct successor of ancient comedy minus the songs. The humor derives from verbal timing (or precise editing), sight gags, and shocking risqué statements. Television sitcom plots are very loose and often make sense only in a week-by-week context. Taken in the long view, sitcom characters are often called upon to behave in very inconsistent manners.

In an acting class designed to teach a student about organic performance, the tricks and blatant theatricality of popular comedy falls into the same category of objectionable behaviors as those listed among Stanislavski's targets in Chapter 2. Some instructors expressly forbid their students from performing comedic pieces during their early training. Even when not explicitly forbidden, students in many classrooms find there is an implicit prohibition because their instructors doubt the material engages the skills of the psychologically based actor. In either case the friction can be palpable between instructors and students because of the latter's widespread and general affection for popular comedy.

There are many subdivisions of comedy, however, not all like the sitcom. Comedy that is based in character, as opposed to relying on jokes, *schtick,* and shock, uses the acting principles derived from Stanislavski and outlined throughout this book in exactly the same way as character-based dramatic material does. In selecting material, one rule of thumb that is frequently effective is to look for comedies by a playwright whose corpus of plays also includes dramatic work, like Terrence McNally, Wendy Wasserstein, or George C. Wolfe.

Having selected comedic material, the major further consideration is to remember that comedy usually brings with it important given circumstances in the forms of characters' obsessions with points of view that they have enough information to realistically abandon but, because of who they are, fail to give up. In the great Irish comedy *The Playboy of the Western World*, a host of characters convince themselves that the central character of the play, Christy Mahon, is heroic despite a wealth of evidence that he is an inexperienced, neurotic adolescent. They want to believe in his heroism and make him into something he is not out of their need for a hero more than out of his actions. Because we can see the difference between our reality and their obsession, we find it funny.

Characters also come with misperceptions about the given circumstances. In the audience we often know a factual piece of information that a character either doesn't know or misunderstands. The given circumstance, therefore, is different for the character than it is for the audience. To play the character convincingly, and humorously, the actor has to commit herself to the character's belief viewpoint in relation to a circumstance that differs from the actor's knowledge. In Shakespeare's *Twelfth Night*, for example, Lady Olivia fails to see through Viola's male disguise and falls in love with her to our amusement and her frustration. (This, of course, is no different in terms of technique than an actor playing Hamlet, for example, being called upon to commit himself to the belief that he can win the crown and become king, even though the actor knows full well the script says he will die without achieving that goal. The effect is tragic, rather than comic, but the actor is doing the same work.)

The most difficult adjustment to the given circumstances in comedy is that many actions do not have the weight or consequence we experience in our everyday world. In many comedies, duels are fought in which we know that not only will no one die but in fact there is little danger that anyone will get hurt. In modern mode, think for a second about the *Home Alone* movies, in which the "bad guys" are endlessly assaulted and maimed, but with mere cartoon consequences. Physical dangers, violence, and illness are only hindrances without long-term effect. In Hugh Leonard's play *Da*, even death does not have finality. The leading character's deceased father follows him around and inserts himself into the life and thoughts of his long-suffering son, apparently unaware that death ordinarily slows down such involvements. These adjustments don't require the actor to behave in unrealistic ways, but to behave realistically within a given circumstance where there is a loosened relationship between cause and effect.

Recommended Reading

These are just a few of the enlightening books available about acting, theatre, and applicable theories arising from the cognitive sciences. They will give you a firm starting point for your studies.

Books by and About Stanislavski and His System

BENEDETTI, JEAN. *Stanislavski: A Biography.* New York: Routledge, 1988. *An excellent biography of Stanislavski and an overview of the development of his system by a distinguished translator of Stanislavski's works.*

BOLESLAVSKY, RICHARD. *Acting: The First Six Lessons.* New York: Theatre Arts, 1933. *A charming, if quaintly sexist, short book by the first great teacher of the system in America. This book is written in the same seminovelistic style as Stanislavski's books on acting. Of all the books on this list, this one is the closest—in subject matter and scope—to the book you are now reading.*

GORDON, MEL. *The Stanislavsky Technique: Russia.* New York: Applause, 1987. *The best summary of the complex development of the Stanislavski system in Russia. This thoroughly documented work covers the major exercises Stanislavski and his protégés actually taught in their studios. Overall, the best introduction available to those trying to sort out all the information on the system. Unfortunately, the planned companion volume on the development of the system in America never reached publication.*

STANISLAVSKI, KONSTANTIN. *An Actor Prepares.* Translated by Elizabeth Reynolds Hapgood. First American edition. New York: Theater Arts, 1936. *The first in a trilogy of acting books by Stanislavski. They are discussed in Chapter 2 of this book.*

STANISLAVSKI, KONSTANTIN. *Building a Character.* Translated by Elizabeth Reynolds Hapgood. First American edition. New York: Theater Arts, 1949. *The second of the three acting books by Stanislavski.*

STANISLAVSKI, KONSTANTIN. *Creating a Role.* Translated by Elizabeth Reynolds Hapgood. First American edition. New York: Theater Arts, 1961. *The final book in Stanislavski's series of acting books.*

STANISLAVSKI, KONSTANTIN. *My Life in Art.* Translated by J. J. Robbins. First American edition. New York: Theater Arts, 1948. *Widely regarded as the final word on Stanislavski's system, this autobiographical exposition is actually a bit misleading. Because Stanislavski was an eclipsingly famous person in his own time, he underplayed both his reputation and his skills. As a result, this book is interesting but incomplete. Read it in combination with Benedetti's biography to better understand its context.*

STANISLAVSKI, KONSTANTIN. *Stanislavsky on the Art of the Stage.* Translated and with an introduction by David Magarshack. London: Faber and Faber, 1950. *A translation of a set of lectures in which Stanislavski presented an overview of his system. Very informative and more concise than the acting books.*

Books by Legendary American Teachers on Their Variations of Stanislavski's Method

ADLER, STELLA. *The Technique of Acting.* New York: Bantam, 1988. *Adler was a student of Boleslavsky, and for a brief time of Stanislavski himself. Her book lacks the clarity and organization of many other books on the system, but as an additional perspective it is valuable.*

HAGEN, UTA. *A Challenge for the Actor.* New York: Charles Scribner's Sons, 1991. *Hagen was America's premiere actress/teacher, long renowned for her studio in New York. This book explains the exercises she taught there. It is a revision of her earlier work* Respect for Acting.

MEISNER, SANFORD, AND DENNIS LONGWELL. *Sanford Meisner on Acting.* New York: Vintage Books (Random House), 1987. *Along with Strasberg and Adler, Meisner was the third great American acting teacher coming from the Group Theater, a legendary American company that won widespread fame for Stanislavski's theory. This book details his adaptations of the method. It is again novelistic in style, rather than a how-to book, but very informative within that format.*

STRASBERG, LEE. *A Dream of Passion: The Development of the Method.* Boston: Little, Brown, 1987. *Probably the most famous, and most controversial, of American acting teachers, Strasberg developed his own version of Stanislavski's system, famously known as the Method. This posthumous book was edited by Evangeline Morphos from his papers explaining the development of his theories.*

Recent American Books on Acting

BARR, TONY. *Acting for the Camera.* New York: Harper and Row, 1982. *A short, extremely practical book about how to apply the principles of the Stanislavski system to screen acting.*

BARTON, ROBERT. *Acting: Onstage and Off.* Third edition. New York: Holt, Reinhart, and Winston, 2003. *Barton's book is an excellent guide to contemporary thinking about acting, written for the novice. His new third edition offers many new, contemporary examples.*

BRUDER, MELISSA, LEE MICHAEL COHN, MADELEINE OLNEK, NATHANIEL POLLACK, ROBERT PREVITO, AND SCOTT ZIGLER, eds. *A Practical Handbook for the Actor.* New York: Vintage Books (Random House), 1986. *This extremely short book is a transcription of playwright David Mamet's lectures on acting. The book addresses a limited number of topics—essentially corresponding to Chapter 11 of this book—but gives many illuminating examples.*

COHEN, ROBERT. *Acting Power.* Palo Alto, CA: Mayfield, 1978. *Though I have come to disagree with its heavy emphasis on logic, I still find this the most inspiring of recent books on acting because of its willingness to think theoretically about what one actually does while acting. Cohen explores a complex range of topics insightfully. His comments on style are the best available explanations. Cohen has written a "lite" version of this book, called* Acting One, *but I prefer the longer book for serious actors.*

SHURTLEFF, MICHAEL. *Audition.* New York: Walker, 1978. *Though this book is specifically about auditioning, it has much to say about acting in general. Shurtleff has become a well-known lecturer on acting because of his pragmatic and easily applied theories.*

Books About Voice, Speech, and Movement

BERRY, CICELY. *The Actor and the Text.* Revised edition. New York: Applause, 1992. *This book by the leading voice teacher in Great Britain addresses advanced techniques of acting and vocal production.*

BERRY, CICELY. *Voice and the Actor.* First American edition. New York: Macmillan, 1974. *Berry's first book sets down the basic principles of vocal production.*

LINKLATER, KRISTIN. *Freeing the Natural Voice.* New York: Drama Book Specialists, 1975. *A book similar to Berry's basic text by the leading American teacher of voice and speech.*

PISK, LITZ. *The Actor and His Body.* New York: Theater Arts, 1987. *Not particularly well known, this is a handy little book introducing body work to the novice.*

RODENBURG, PATSY. *The Need for Words: Voice and the Text.* London: Routledge, 1993. *A basic book on voice and speech. Especially good for students with vocal difficulties.*

RODENBURG, PATSY. *The Right to Speak: Working with the Voice.* New York: Theater Arts, 1993. *The theory behind Rodenburg's previous book. This is a strong feminist argument for voice work as personal empowerment.*

Books About the Brain, the Mind, Thought, the Senses, and Art

ACKERMAN, DIANE. *A Natural History of the Senses.* New York: Vintage Books (Random House), 1990. *Six related essays celebrating each of the senses, in turn, and culminating with a view of synesthesia—a rare but artistically related sensory phenomenon.*

BODEN, MARGARET A. *The Creative Mind: Myths and Mechanisms.* New York: Basic Books (HarperCollins), 1990. *A look at the cognitive sciences, the arts, and their interrelationships.*

CAMPBELL, JEREMY. *The Improbable Machine.* New York: Simon and Schuster, 1989. *The single best book available on artificial intelligence and what it reveals about the human mind. Campbell's earlier book* Grammatical Man *contains a particularly illuminating chapter on the split-brain phenomenon.*

CYTOWIC, RICHARD E., M.D. *The Man Who Tasted Shapes.* With new afterword. Cambridge, MA: MIT Press, 2003. *This revision of Cytowic's 1993 book on people with synesthesia is illuminating for its primary subject matter but also delves into many related artistic phenomena. It also has much to say about work with the senses in people who do not have this rare neurological condition.*

DAMASIO, ANTONIO. *The Feeling of What Happens.* San Diego: Harcourt, Inc., 1999. *An extraordinarily insightful book about the emotional process inside the human mind. Through this and his other books,* Descartes' Error *and* Looking for Spinoza, *Damasio has become recognized as the leading writer on emotion and cognition for a general audience.*

EDWARDS, BETTY. *The New Drawing on the Right Side of the Brain.* Second Edition. Los Angeles: Jeremy P. Tarcher, 1999. *This is the best-selling art book of all time, using cognitive theory to illuminate art instruction. Highly recommended for beginning artists in all disciplines. The sequel to this book,* Drawing on the Artist Within, *also has intriguing insights about artistic issues.*

FREEDMAN, DAVID H. *Brainmakers: How Scientists Are Moving Beyond Computers to Create a Rival to the Human Brain.* New York: Simon and Schuster, 1994. *A recent look at the advances in artificial intelligence research.*

GARDNER, HOWARD. *Creating Minds.* New York: Basic Books (HarperCollins), 1993. *By the creator of the theory of multiple intelligences, this superb book looks at the lives and ideas of artistic geniuses.*

GARDNER, HOWARD. *Frames of Mind.* New York: Basic Books (HarperCollins), 1985. *This book by the director of Harvard's Project Zero focuses on the broad range of capabilities of the human mind and accords a particular intellectual respect to the arts.*

HUMPHREY, NICHOLAS. *A History of the Mind.* New York: HarperPerennial (HarperCollins), 1992. *This evolutionary argument about the development of the human mind casts interesting light on the thought pyramid as a reflection of the actual layers of the brain.*

JOHNSON, STEVEN. *Emergence: The Connected Lives of Ants, Brains, Cities and Software.* New York: Scribner, 2001. *In the most interesting brain book of the new century, Johnson explains the layers of the brain with uncommon clarity in order to discuss the complex phenomenon that makes an anthill smarter than any ant living in it, and our total mental capacity greater than our conscious awareness.*

LANGER, SUSANNE K. *Form and Feeling: A Theory of Art Developed from "Philosophy in a New Key."* New York: Charles Scribner's Sons, 1953. *Though of a different vintage than any other book in this section, this classic book on aesthetics still has much to say about the way the arts reveal the human mind.*

MILLER, JONATHAN. *States of Mind.* New York: Pantheon, 1983. *The author of this book is not only a medical doctor but a well-known stage director and actor. His book explores mental states and phenomena from a medical perspective, but he often directs penetrating questions with a theatrical basis to some of the world's leading cognitive scientists. The chapter on emotion is particularly theatrical.*

PINKER, STEVEN. *How the Mind Works.* New York: W. W. Norton, 1997. *A national best-seller, this book is especially good at explaining how science is revealing the operations of the mind below the conscious level. It is a great companion piece for any student studying acting to learn more about him- or herself. Pinker's recent work,* The Blank Slate, *is also recommended.*

SPRINGER, SALLY P., AND GEORG DEUTSCH. *Left Brain, Right Brain.* Fifth edition. New York: W. H. Freeman, 1997. *The best book available on the split-brain phenomenon and the research available on this topic. Encyclopedic coverage of all the issues related to left and right hemisphere functioning, kept up-to-date in recent editions.*

pilogue

This book has gone as far as it intended to go—it has taught you about the thought processes that underlie acting. The journey was meant to be rewarding in itself. Our mind is so rich and fertile that the exploration of its possibilities can be engaging with no thought of further application.

However, you may want to know more about theatre generally and acting specifically. If that is the case, here are some ideas about what steps you might take next.

There are three acting areas left to explore in depth. The first is the application of these principles to nonrealistic styles and to other media. Some of the most exciting and intriguing theatre is not written to resemble or reflect the world as we usually experience it. It is abstract. When working in these alternative worlds, with their unique assumptions and unusual rules, the actor's fundamental thought processes do not change. The creative state will be as applicable as ever. There will, however, be many new aspects of performance, sometimes completely altering the basic conventions and expectations about what we are doing. With a good director or instructor these nonrealistic scenes will open new and wonderfully rewarding vistas for you.

Likewise, working in film and television uses the creative state, but the process of rehearsing and presenting a performance is considerably altered because of the differences between film and theatre. As just one example, the story in film is not necessarily performed in the order that it will be presented later. It would be as if you were performing a scene from act 3 followed by a quick jump back to act 1 and finishing with a flourish from act 2. The creative process does not change, but the surface conditions do.

The second area might be a fuller, deeper exploration of characterization. Playing characters who are very unlike you in temperament, age, or appearance involves the principles outlined in this book but extends them. The process of characterization can involve learning and then varying your physical patterns, your vocal habits, and your mental perspectives. It is fascinating study.

The final area for future study is style, particularly historic styles used in presenting theatre works from the past. My own area of specialty, for example, is Shakespearean performance. Plays from great periods of theatre history are mind expanding, challenging, and (don't let the secret out) fun. To learn to speak verse with conviction, to learn to adopt the customs and manners of other times, and to learn about the philosophical and moral questions that concerned other ages requires advanced study. Again, you will find the creative state is applicable, but the process will be augmented and extended.

The theatre is a big field with aspects that reach far beyond acting. You might find the creative processes of collaborative artists, like designers, directors, and dramaturgs, intriguing in ways relating to what you have already learned. The history of the theatre, reaching back as far as recorded history, is study worth your time and effort.

It is also possible that you will want to consider a professional career. This will not be easy. It requires solid technique, great dedication, and tenacity. I cannot cover even a sliver of the information you will need to collect, but I believe that theatrical study will serve you well in your life whether or not a career eventually emerges from your efforts. I urge you to enter it with the same spirit of discovery and excitement that guided you through this book. Good luck, and welcome!

# Notes

Page 3, Zelda Fichlander, in Arthur Bartow, *The Director's Voice*, New York: Theater Communications Group, 1987.

Page 3, Anne Bancroft, in Lewis Funke and John E. Booth, *Actors Talk About Acting*, New York: Avon, 1961.

Page 4, Richard Hornby, *The End of Acting: A Radical View*, New York: Applause Books, 1992, p. 65.

Page 17, Mel Gordon, *The Stanislavsky Technique: Russia*. New York: Applause Books, 1987, p. 28.

Page 18, Stanislavski, in Jean Benedetti, *Stanislavski: A Biography*, New York: Routledge, 1988, pp. 191–92.

Page 19, David Magarshack, *Stanislavsky on the Art of the Stage*, London: Faber and Faber, 1950.

Page 22, Stanislavski, in Jean Benedetti, *Stanislavski: A Biography*, p. 194.

Page 23, Mel Gordon, *The Stanislavsky Technique: Russia*, p. xii.

Page 32, Betty Edwards, *Drawing on the Right Side of the Brain*, Los Angeles: Jeremy P. Tarcher, 1989, p. 27.

Page 34, Brad Leithauser, "No Loyalty to DNA," *The New Yorker,* 9 January 1989, p. 84.

Page 35, Jeremy Campbell, *The Improbable Machine*, New York: Simon and Schuster, 1989, p. 32.

Page 39, Diane Ackerman, *A Natural History of the Senses*, New York: Vintage Books (Random House), 1990, p. 20.

Page 51, Tony Barr, *Acting for the Camera*, New York: Perennial Library (Harper and Row), 1982, p. 20.

Page 52, Richard Hornby, *The End of Acting: A Radical View,* p. 80.

Page 54, Diane Ackerman, *A Natural History of the Senses,* p. 233.

Page 56, Dale Moffit, in Eva Mekler, *The New Generation of Acting Teachers,* New York: Penguin Books, 1987, p. 369.

Page 65, Jeremy Campbell, *The Improbable Machine,* p. 16.

Page 69, Jeremy Campbell, *The Improbable Machine,* p. 35.

Page 88, Steven Pinker, *The Language Instinct,* New York: HarperPerennial (HarperCollins), 1994, p. 67.

Page 95, Steven Pinker, *The Language Instinct,* p. 57.

Page 105, Stephen Spinella, in Janet Sonenberg, *The Actor Speaks,* New York: Crown Trade Paperbacks, 1996, p. 283.

Page 106, Tony Barr, *Acting for the Camera,* p. 79.

Page 126, Warren Robertson, in Eva Mekler, *The New Generation of Acting Teachers,* p. 121.

Page 132, Dianne Wiest, in Janet Sonenberg, *The Actor Speaks,* p. 262.

Page 140, David Mamet, *Writing in Restaurants,* New York: Viking, 1986, p. 28.

Page 142, Olympia Dukakis, in Janet Sonenberg, *The Actor Speaks,* p. 304.

Page 146, Richard Hornby, *The End of Acting: A Radical View,* p. 73.

Page 149, Tony Barr, *Acting for the Camera,* p. 114.

Page 170, Stephen Spinella, in Janet Sonenberg, *The Actor Speaks,* p. 277.

Page 177, Anthony Zerbe, in Susan Shacter and Don Shewey, *Caught in the Act,* New York: New American Library, 1986, p. 191.

Page 181, Diane Ackerman, *A Natural History of the Senses,* p. 6.

Page 181, Olympia Dukakis, in Janet Sonenberg, *The Actor Speaks,* p. 301.

Figure Credits

Figure 1.1: Photograph courtesy of Rosemary Ingham.
Figure 1.2: Photograph courtesy of Jack Pleasants.
Figure 1.3: Photograph courtesy of Rosemary Ingham.
Figure 1.4: From an 1898 text on public speaking and performing called *The Speaker's Ideal Entertainments.*
Figure 1.5: Joan Marcus photograph, courtesy of the Arena Theater.
Figure 2.1: Photograph courtesy of the Billy Rose Theatre Collection, The New York Public Library for the Performing Arts, Astor, Lenox, and Tilden Foundations.
Figure 2.2: Photograph courtesy of the Billy Rose Theatre Collection, The New York Public Library for the Performing Arts, Astor, Lenox, and Tilden Foundations.
Figure 2.3: Photograph courtesy of the Billy Rose Theatre Collection, The New York Public Library for the Performing Arts, Astor, Lenox, and Tilden Foundations.
Figure 3.1: Drawing by Lawren Spera, based on information found in Richard Restak, M.D., *The Brain,* New York: Bantam Books, 1984.
Figure 3.2, Figure 3.3, Figure 3.4: Drawings by Lawren Spera.
Figure 4.1: Photograph courtesy of Rosemary Ingham.
Figure 4.2: Drawing by Lawren Spera.
Page 63: *Portrait of Igor Stravinsky,* by Pablo Picasso (1881–1973), dated 21 May 1920, Paris. Privately owned. © 1997 Estate of Pablo Picasso/Artists Rights Society (ARS), New York.
Figure 9.1: Photograph of the Long Wharf Theater production of *Mother Courage,* courtesy of Rosemary Ingham.
Figure 9.2: Richard Feldman photograph, courtesy of the Arena Theater.
Figure 10.1: Photograph of the Court Theater (Beloit College) production of *The Winslow Boy,* courtesy of Rosemary Ingham.
Figure 11.1: Photograph of the Long Wharf Theater production of *Mother Courage,* courtesy of Rosemary Ingham.
Figure 12.1: Photograph courtesy of Rosemary Ingham.

Index